WHY AI FAILS

WHY AI FAILS

The Leadership Discipline Behind the 5% Who Succeed

Neil D. Morris

Authentic Tech Leadership LLC

Colorado

Why AI Fails: The Leadership Discipline Behind the 5% Who Succeed

Copyright © 2026 by Neil D. Morris

Published by Authentic Tech Leadership LLC

www.whyaifails.com

First Edition: March 2026

Library of Congress Control Number: 2026906481

ISBN-13:

- 979-8-9950294-0-3 (Paperback)

- 979-8-9950294-1-0 (Hardcover)

- 979-8-9950294-2-7 (eBook)

Printed in the United States of America

10 9 8 7 6 5 4 3 2 1

Legal Disclaimer:

A Note on Case Studies and Examples:

The case studies and examples throughout this book are drawn from extensive research into real-world AI initiatives—published case studies, industry reports, academic research, and documented organizational outcomes. Some scenarios are drawn directly from documented cases with identifying details changed. Others are composite illustrations synthesized from patterns documented across dozens of organizations. Specific details—company names, financial figures, and individual roles—have been modified to protect confidentiality while preserving the essential patterns and strategic lessons. Unless otherwise noted, named individuals in case studies are composite characters representing patterns observed across multiple leaders and organizations. All frameworks, assessments, and recommendations reflect documented industry patterns and research.

To the teams I've had the honor to lead—
You demonstrated daily that organizational capability
matters more than individual heroics.
This book is about what I learned from you.

TABLE OF CONTENTS

Why AI Fails: The Leadership Discipline Behind the 5% Who Succeed

How to Use This Book

Introduction: The $40 Billion Failure

PART I: THE LANDSCAPE

Chapter 1: The $40 Billion Question

Chapter 2: Why Leadership, Not Technology

Chapter 3: The Bubble Reality

PART II: THE SEVEN PILLARS

Chapter 4: Strategic Clarity—The North Star Principle

Chapter 5: Leadership Alignment—Building the Coalition

Chapter 6: Capability Building—The Permanent Asset

Chapter 7: Pilot Discipline—The Experimentation Framework

Chapter 8: Scale Strategy—From Pilot to Production

Chapter 9: Risk Management—Building Guardrails That Enable

Chapter 10: Continuous Evolution—The Learning Discipline

PART III: PUTTING IT INTO PRACTICE

Chapter 11: The Asset-Liability Assessment—Transforming Framework Into Action

Chapter 12: From Assessment to Action—The 30-60-90 Day Transformation Framework

Chapter 13: Measuring What Matters—The Three-Layer Metrics Framework for AI Portfolio Health

Chapter 14: Building Your AI-Ready Organization—The Architecture of Lasting Competitive Advantage

PART IV: THE PATH FORWARD

Chapter 15: The Long Game

Chapter 16: The Leadership Imperative—The Rare Discipline That Separates Success from Failure

Resources Guide

Seven Pillars Quick Reference

About The Author

References & Bibliography

Acknowledgments

Connect

Also From Neil D. Morris

How To Use This Book

This book is designed for busy executives who need both strategic understanding and practical implementation guidance. Here's how to get the most from it:

For the Time-Constrained Executive

If you have two hours: Read the Introduction and Part IV (Chapters 15–16). You'll understand the problem, why it matters, and what to do about it.

If you have a full day: Read the Introduction, skim Part I for context, deep-dive Part II (The Seven Pillars), and read Chapter 11 (The Asset-Liability Assessment). You'll have the complete strategic framework.

If you're implementing now: Start with Chapter 12 (From Assessment to Action), then work backward through the Seven Pillars to address your specific gaps.

Book Structure

Part I: The Landscape frames the problem. You'll learn why 95% of AI initiatives fail and why this is a leadership challenge, not a technology problem. If you're skeptical about AI transformation, start here.

Part II: The Seven Pillars delivers the strategic framework. These seven disciplines—from Strategic Clarity through Continuous Evolution—form the foundation of successful transformation. Each pillar is independent yet interconnected. Read in sequence or jump to your greatest weakness.

Part III: Putting It Into Practice translates framework into action. The Asset-Liability Assessment (Chapter 11) gives you a lens for evaluating every AI initiative. Chapter 12 maps the path from assessment to action with a concrete 30-60-90 day framework. Chapter 13 shows you how to measure what matters. Chapter 14 defines what an AI-ready organization looks like and the decade-long path to building one.

Part IV: The Path Forward addresses the bigger picture. How do you manage market uncertainty? How do you build capability that lasts decades, not months? What does authentic leadership look like in the AI era?

Digital Resources

Throughout the book, you'll find references to digital resources—assessment tools, templates, extended frameworks, and implementation guides. These are available at:

www.whyaifails.com

The digital resources aren't required—the book stands alone—but they accelerate implementation. Register with your email to access the complete toolkit: assessment tools, templates, extended frameworks, and implementation guides.

A Note on Reading Style

This isn't a reference manual to memorize. It's a practitioner's guide designed to change how you think about transformation.

Read it with a pen. Mark up the assessments. Dog-ear the frameworks you'll use Monday morning. Skip sections that don't apply to your context. Come back to chapters as challenges emerge.

Above all: don't try to implement everything at once. Pick your highest-leverage starting point (Chapter 12 will help) and build from there.

The goal isn't perfection across all Seven Pillars immediately. The goal is disciplined, sustained progress that compounds over time.

That's how the 5% succeed where the 95% fail.

The $40 Billion Failure

Two financial services organizations. Same industry, same year, same AI technology. One spent $3.2 million on a customer service chatbot that ran for two years as a pilot, never reached production, and delivered zero business value. The other spent $400,000, reached full production in six months, and saved $1.9 million in its first year. The difference wasn't the AI. It wasn't the budget. It was leadership discipline—the systematic execution of fundamentals that one organization practiced and the other skipped entirely. Chapter 1 tells their full story, but their divergence captures the central paradox of enterprise AI today.

The evidence behind that paradox is damning. Research from MIT, McKinsey, and RAND Corporation converges on the same conclusion: somewhere between 80% and 95% of enterprise AI initiatives fail to deliver measurable business value, depending on scope and definition. MIT's Project NANDA found in its 2025 "GenAI Divide" report that 95% of organizations investing in generative AI saw no measurable return on their P&L. McKinsey reported that fewer than one in three organizations have begun scaling AI programs, with only a small fraction achieving enterprise-wide impact. RAND found that more than 80% of AI projects fail outright—twice the rate of non-AI IT projects.

Not disappointing returns. Not marginal gains. Zero.

The 95% figure specifically addresses generative AI initiatives —the newest and most hyped category—while the McKinsey and RAND research spans all enterprise AI. The precise numbers differ by scope, but the pattern is consistent and the range is narrow enough to be damning: the overwhelming majority of AI investments fail to deliver.

Organizations are investing between $30 and $40 billion annually in AI initiatives—and more than nine in ten of those investments generate zero measurable return. Hyperscalers are projected to invest $400 billion in AI infrastructure in 2025 alone —more than the entire inflation-adjusted cost of the Apollo program. OpenAI pursues valuations approaching $500 billion while remaining unprofitable. Its CEO acknowledges we're in a phase where "investors as a whole are overexcited about AI."

This is the paradox defining AI today: transformative technology meeting spectacular implementation failure.

Why Smart Organizations Keep Failing

Here's what should terrify every technology leader: the organizations failing at AI aren't incompetent. They're not under-resourced. They're not unsophisticated.

They're organizations like yours.

Fortune 500 companies with deep pockets and experienced leadership teams. Organizations that successfully executed previous technology transformations. Teams that understand cloud, cybersecurity, digital transformation. Leaders who survived the dot-com bubble, the mobile revolution, the shift to SaaS.

Yet they're failing at AI at rates never seen in previous technology cycles.

The reason isn't technical—it's foundational. Organizations treat AI as a technology problem when it's a leadership problem. They chase sophisticated solutions while neglecting execution fundamentals. They optimize for demonstrations over deployment, for vendor relationships over internal capability, for activity over outcomes.

They're building expensive technical debt disguised as strategic assets.

After twenty-five years leading enterprise IT transformations across private and public organizations in aerospace, defense, energy, and technology—I've watched this pattern repeat through every major technology shift. Cloud migration, cybersecurity transformation, digital modernization. The organizations that succeed don't win by adopting technology first or spending the most. They win by mastering the leadership fundamentals that make technology adoption effective.

What's changed with AI is the consequences of getting these fundamentals wrong.

AI amplifies everything—the advantages of disciplined execution and the costs of undisciplined implementation alike. Get the basics right and AI creates compound advantages that persist for decades. Get them wrong and AI accelerates your organization's decline while consuming millions in capital.

What Discipline Means in This Book

Throughout these pages, I use one word more than any other: *discipline*. It deserves a precise definition, because I don't mean it casually.

Discipline is the systematic execution of fundamentals under organizational pressure to do otherwise.

Not rigor for rigor's sake. Not process for process's sake. Discipline means doing what works—building strategic clarity, aligning leadership, developing internal capability, killing zombie pilots, managing risk—when every force in the organization pushes you toward what's exciting, what's easy, or what looks good in a board presentation.

The martial arts parallel is deliberate. I've trained for decades, and the lesson that transfers most directly to technology leadership is this: perfect execution of basics under pressure beats sophisticated techniques executed poorly. Every single time. The black belt doesn't signal mastery of advanced moves. It signals fundamentals perfected so thoroughly that advanced moves become possible.

The organizations in the 5% aren't smarter or better funded. They're more disciplined about fundamentals. That's the entire thesis of this book.

The Stakes Are Higher Than You Think

Most discussions about AI failure focus on wasted investment. That's real—$40 billion collectively is roughly $100 to $200 million for a typical large enterprise over two years. But wasted capital is the smallest consequence of AI failure.

The real cost is opportunity loss. Every month spent on poorly scoped pilots is a month competitors use to build actual capability. Every dollar invested in vendor dependencies rather than internal expertise is a dollar that could have built permanent organizational assets. Every hour a leader spends on AI theater rather than AI transformation is time stolen from building sustainable competitive advantage.

You can't get that time back. The correction that's coming—and everyone from Sam Altman to Morgan Stanley analysts acknowledges it—will expose which organizations built real capability and which built expensive facades.

And here's what should concern every technology leader: most organizations don't know which category they're in. They're measuring AI success by demos deployed, vendors engaged, pilots launched. They think they're building assets when they're actually accumulating liabilities that will compound and eventually require expensive unwinding.

Who Should Read This Book

This book is for technology leaders who sense something is wrong with their AI programs but can't articulate what. Leaders who feel pressure to show progress but question whether their initiatives build anything sustainable. Executives who understand AI is transformative but struggle to translate that understanding into organizational results.

If you're a CIO, CTO, or technology executive responsible for AI strategy and you're being honest with yourself, you probably recognize these warning signs:

Your AI pilots rarely make it to production. When they do, they require constant vendor support to remain operational. Your costs per AI initiative are increasing rather than decreasing. You're building expertise in vendors rather than your organization. You have more zombie pilots consuming resources without generating value than you'd like to admit. Your AI governance process is either non-existent or creates such friction that teams work around it.

Most telling: you can't articulate your AI strategy in sixty seconds without jargon, and you're not confident your executive team could either.

These aren't signs of incompetence—they're signs you're doing what everyone else does. And what everyone else does produces those failure rates.

This book offers a different path.

A Note on Case Studies

A word about the stories in this book. The case studies and examples in these pages are drawn from extensive research into real-world AI initiatives across industries—published case studies, industry reports, academic research, and documented organizational outcomes.

To illustrate common patterns, I use several approaches throughout the book. Some scenarios are drawn directly from documented cases with identifying details changed. Others— including composite characters like Sarah Chen in the final chapter—synthesize patterns observed repeatedly across multiple organizations into single illustrative narratives.

Every pattern described in this book reflects real organizational dynamics documented in research and industry reporting. The failure patterns, success trajectories, and financial figures reflect actual outcomes across aerospace, defense, energy, financial services, and enterprise technology. Where I've composited multiple cases into one narrative, the underlying dynamics are no less real for being combined.

What This Book Delivers

This is not a book about AI technology. You won't find chapters on transformers, RAG architectures, or fine-tuning. Plenty of technical books exist for that.

This is a book about the leadership discipline required to succeed with AI regardless of which technologies dominate. The frameworks here work whether GPT-7 revolutionizes the field next year or we're still using today's models in 2030.

Part I: The Landscape establishes context. Chapter 1 details the $40 billion question—why organizations are failing despite massive investment. Chapter 2 explains why AI success is fundamentally a leadership problem, not a technology problem. Chapter 3 addresses the bubble dynamics and how to build capability regardless of when the correction comes.

Part II: The Seven Pillars provides deep exploration of foundational disciplines every AI program requires. Strategic Clarity before activity. Leadership Alignment before resource commitment. Capability Building as permanent asset. Pilot Discipline that kills zombie projects. Scale Strategy that actually moves from pilot to production. Risk Management that enables rather than blocks innovation. Continuous Evolution that compounds capability over time.

Each pillar chapter includes diagnostic questions revealing where your organization stands, specific actions to improve capability, common failure patterns to avoid, and frameworks for sustainable implementation.

Part III: Putting It Into Practice delivers practical tools. The Asset-Liability Framework helps you evaluate whether AI investments build capability or accumulate technical debt. The 30-60-90 Day Action Plan provides immediate next steps. Measurement frameworks track what matters rather than what's easy to count. The AI-Ready Organization chapter shows how to build capability that persists across technology generations.

Part IV: The Path Forward addresses the long game. How to build compound capability advantage over years and decades. How to sustain focus when everyone else optimizes for quarterly results. How to maintain leadership discipline when pressure mounts to chase trends.

The Path Starts Here

If you're reading this book, you sense your AI program isn't delivering what it should. You've launched pilots that never scale. You've spent millions without clear returns. You've felt pressure to demonstrate progress while questioning whether you're building anything sustainable.

You're not alone. You're in the 95%.

But you don't have to stay there.

The organizations that succeed at AI—the rare few who translate investment into competitive advantage—aren't smarter, better funded, or more technically sophisticated. They're more disciplined about fundamentals.

Chapter 1 starts with the $40 billion question—why do organizations fail despite massive investment? Once you understand the dynamics driving that failure rate, everything else falls into place. The Seven Pillars aren't arbitrary—they're the specific disciplines that distinguish the organizations that succeed from those that fail.

You can read this book cover to cover, or skip directly to the pillar chapters that address your most urgent gaps. You can implement the full transformation roadmap or start with quick wins that build momentum.

But you can't ignore the fundamentals and expect different results from what the overwhelming majority of organizations are experiencing.

The AI revolution is real. The transformation is inevitable. But success won't come from chasing the latest models or spending the most on infrastructure.

It will come from mastering the basics.

PART I: THE LANDSCAPE

The $40 Billion Question

Forty billion dollars. That's the estimated annual cost of AI initiatives that fail to deliver promised value. Behind that number lie thousands of organizations—from Fortune 100 enterprises to ambitious startups—that started with enthusiasm, invested heavily, and ended with little to show beyond vendor invoices and exhausted teams.

The failure rate I mentioned in the introduction isn't hyperbole. The range across major studies is 80–95%, depending on scope and how failure is defined. MIT's Project NANDA found in its 2025 "GenAI Divide" report that despite $30 to $40 billion invested in generative AI, 95% of organizations saw no measurable return on their P&L—the highest failure rate, likely because generative AI is the newest and least understood category. A 2024 RAND Corporation study found that more than 80% of AI projects fail—twice the rate of non-AI IT projects. Gartner predicted in 2018 that through 2022, 85% of AI projects would deliver erroneous outcomes—a prediction subsequent research broadly confirmed. The pattern holds across industries, company sizes, and geographies. Whether you're implementing computer vision in manufacturing, natural language processing (NLP) in customer service, or predictive analytics in supply chain, the odds of delivering measurable ROI are roughly the same as flipping a coin five times and getting heads every time.

But here's the part that demands attention: these aren't technology failures. Every zombie pilot documented in the research had functioning AI. The models worked. The algorithms performed as designed. The infrastructure scaled.

The organizations failed because they treated AI as a technology problem when it is fundamentally a leadership challenge.

The Scale of Waste

Here is what $40 billion in annual AI waste means in practice.

Individual AI pilot failures typically cost between $500,000 and $2 million, with complex implementations reaching $5 million or more. McKinsey's State of AI research consistently finds that fewer than one in three organizations have begun scaling AI programs—leaving the majority burning budget without delivering business value.

My $40 billion estimate is conservative. It draws on the MIT NANDA finding of $30 to $40 billion invested with 95% generating zero measurable return, and it counts only direct technology spending—excluding the opportunity cost of talented teams trapped in failing initiatives.

The waste shows up in predictable patterns:

Zombie Pilots: AI initiatives that run indefinitely without clear success criteria or go/no-go decisions. Organizations accumulate them like digital hoarding—each consuming monthly cloud compute costs, data science hours, and stakeholder attention while delivering no production value. Industry data shows the average pilot lifespan is nine to twelve months, with many running two years or longer.

Vendor Lock-in: Organizations discover too late that they've built expensive dependencies on proprietary platforms rather than internal capabilities. When they attempt to switch vendors or bring capabilities in-house, migration costs frequently exceed original implementation investments by three to five times.

Strategic Drift: Leadership launches AI initiatives without clear business objectives, allowing projects to proliferate across business units without coordination. One Fortune 100 company ran 47 separate AI pilots with 23 different vendors—and couldn't articulate a coherent strategy connecting any of them to business priorities.

Capability Gaps: Organizations invest millions in AI technology while building zero internal expertise. They can demonstrate capabilities but can't explain how the systems work, can't evaluate alternatives, and can't maintain them without external support.

The deepest damage isn't financial. It's organizational.

Why Smart Organizations Keep Failing

Here's the puzzle: these aren't unsophisticated organizations making rookie mistakes. These are Fortune 500 companies with decades of technology transformation experience. They've navigated ERP implementations, cloud migrations, and digital transformations. They employ brilliant technologists, experienced project managers, and strategic consultants.

Yet AI transformation defeats them with stunning consistency.

Why?

Because AI amplifies everything. Good leadership produces technology success; poor leadership guarantees technology failure. AI widens that gap—exponentially and faster than any previous technology cycle.

Consider two organizations operating in the same year—both mid-sized financial services firms, both implementing customer service chatbots, both using similar technology stacks. Their kickoff meetings happened within weeks of each other. The contrast is striking.

Organization A launched without strategic goals beyond "use AI in customer service." In their kickoff, the conference room buzzed with vendor slides and executive enthusiasm. Not one person asked what specific problem they were solving. They hired consultants to evaluate vendors, selected a platform based on feature comparisons, and began a pilot with 5,000 customers. Six months in, usage sat below 15%, satisfaction scores were mixed, and the team couldn't articulate next steps. The pilot continued for another eighteen months, consuming $3.2 million before being quietly deprecated. Total business value delivered: zero.

Organization B started differently. In their kickoff, a whiteboard dominated the room with three columns: biggest cost drivers, addressability, and data readiness. The CIO opened with a different question: "What specific customer service cost is highest and most addressable?" Answer: password resets and basic account questions consuming 42% of call center volume at

$8.50 per interaction. Reducing this volume by 50% would save $2.4 million annually. They selected AI technology to address this problem, launched a pilot with clear success thresholds (40% volume reduction, 4.0+ satisfaction), and scheduled a go/no-go decision at ninety days. The pilot met all criteria. They scaled to production within six months. Year-one return: $1.9 million saved against $400,000 investment.

Same industry. Same AI capability. Same technology platforms.

Radically different outcomes.

The difference wasn't the AI. It was leadership discipline.

Organization A treated AI as innovation theater. Organization B treated it as business transformation guided by disciplined execution of fundamentals.

This pattern repeats across failed AI initiatives documented in research and industry reporting. Organizations fail in predictable, preventable ways—not through bad luck or insufficient technology, but through specific leadership gaps.

The Five Failure Patterns

Across hundreds of documented failed AI initiatives, five patterns account for most of the $40 billion waste:

Pattern 1: Strategic Confusion

Organizations launch AI initiatives without clear business objectives.

In 2024, a healthcare system audited its AI portfolio. It had fourteen active pilots across diagnostic imaging, patient scheduling, medication optimization, readmission prediction, and clinical documentation. When the board asked the CIO what business problem justified this investment, he said: "We need to stay competitive in healthcare innovation."

That's not a strategy. That's competitive anxiety dressed up as strategy.

Real strategy means choosing what *not* to do. It means prioritizing the few problems whose solution would materially improve financial performance or reduce significant risk. It means articulating in five minutes why you're investing in AI, what specific business outcomes you expect, and how you'll know if you've succeeded.

Strategic clarity requires answering five questions:

1. What specific business problem costs us the most?
2. Could AI meaningfully address this problem?
3. What would success look like in measurable terms?
4. What capabilities must we build versus buy?
5. What are we explicitly choosing not to pursue?

Most organizations can't answer even three of these questions clearly. They're doing AI because competitors are doing AI. Because boards are asking about AI. Because technology vendors are pitching AI solutions.

This is how organizations waste millions: building sophisticated solutions to problems they haven't clearly defined.

Pattern 2: Vendor Dependence Disguised as Partnership

Organizations treat AI as something to buy rather than capability to build.

The pitch is seductive: "Use our pre-trained models and proven platforms rather than building from scratch. You'll get to market faster with less risk."

True enough. But what happens when:

- The vendor raises prices 25% annually because you're locked in?
- Your competitive advantage requires customization the vendor won't support?
- The vendor's roadmap diverges from your strategic needs?
- New vendors offer better technology but migration would require rebuilding everything?

A Fortune 500 retailer learned this the hard way. After three years and $18 million invested in vendor-developed AI systems for inventory management, pricing optimization, and fraud detection, they had built zero internal capability. When their pricing optimization system generated bizarre recommendations, no one in-house could diagnose the problem. They waited three weeks for vendor support while losing millions in margin.

Worse: when they evaluated switching to a different vendor, they discovered migration costs would exceed original implementation by 300%. They were locked in, with annual costs increasing 15 to 20% each year.

This is how strategic AI investments become permanent vendor liabilities.

I'm not arguing against using vendors—that would be absurd. But there's a critical difference between strategic partnerships where you maintain control and dependencies where vendors control your competitive capabilities. Chapter 6 provides a complete framework for building vendor relationships that strengthen your organization rather than capture it.

Pattern 3: The Zombie Pilot Epidemic

Organizations launch pilots with no clear decision framework for scaling or killing them.

A conversation that plays out in boardrooms across the Fortune 100—sometimes in strategy reviews, sometimes at industry conferences—captures the pattern:

"How many AI pilots are you running?"

"Twenty-three active initiatives across various business units."

"How many have reached production?"

"We're still in the learning phase. Several show promise."

"How long has your oldest pilot been running?"

[Long pause] "About two and a half years. But we're gathering valuable lessons."

"What are the go/no-go criteria for scaling versus killing?"

[Longer pause] "We haven't really formalized that. Each team is iterating toward their own definition of success."

This is the death spiral.

Pilots run indefinitely because no one established clear criteria for success or failure. The pilot becomes permanent—consuming resources without delivering production value, not quite successful enough to scale but not obviously failing enough to kill.

Organizations accumulate these "zombie pilots" because:

- No one defines go/no-go criteria upfront
- Killing a pilot requires admitting failure (career risk)
- Sunk cost fallacy: "We've invested so much, we should keep going"
- Any result can be reframed as "learning" rather than failure
- No one has authority to kill initiatives crossing organizational boundaries

The pattern holds across industries: the vast majority of AI pilots never reach production, average pilot duration exceeds 12 months, and organizations typically run far more pilots than they can support effectively.

The waste is staggering—not just financially but in opportunity cost. Every dollar trapped in zombie pilots is a dollar stolen from initiatives that could deliver real value.

Pattern 4: Capability Theater

Organizations invest millions in AI technology while building zero internal expertise.

This is the most insidious pattern because it looks like success —at first. The organization deploys functioning AI systems.

Vendors provide support. Consultants handle technical challenges. Everything appears to work.

Until it doesn't.

When systems need updating, no one internally understands how. When performance degrades, diagnosis requires external help. When new opportunities arise, evaluation requires hiring consultants. When vendors raise prices or change terms, you negotiate from dependency rather than strength.

A financial services company spent $18 million over four years on AI initiatives. When leadership finally assessed their capability, they found:

- Eight systems in production, all vendor-maintained
- Twelve data scientists focused on research projects, not production systems
- Zero ability to maintain existing systems without vendor support
- No framework for evaluating vendor claims or alternative approaches
- Annual costs increasing 18% while business value remained flat

They'd spent $18 million and built no institutional capability. They had impressive demos but depended entirely on vendors for everything that mattered.

This is what happens when organizations treat AI as technology to deploy rather than capability to build.

Pattern 5: Measurement Theater

Organizations measure what's easy instead of what matters.

This pattern appears in AI initiative reviews across industries:

"Our model achieved 94% accuracy on the test set."

"We reduced prediction error by 23% versus the baseline."

"User satisfaction scores averaged 4.2 out of 5."

These are technology metrics. They say nothing about business value.

The questions that matter:

- Did customer service costs decrease?
- Did sales conversion improve?
- Did inventory carrying costs decline?
- Did fraud losses reduce?

But business impact is harder to measure and often disappointing compared to technical metrics. So organizations report what makes them look good rather than what creates value.

This creates a vicious cycle: pilots continue indefinitely because any technical improvement can justify additional investment—even when business value remains zero. Chapter 13 provides the measurement framework that breaks this cycle.

> **RED FLAG: The Innovation Theater Warning**
> Your AI initiative is already theater, not transformation, if:
> - You can't articulate specific business value in one sentence
> - Success is defined as "learning" or "exploring" rather than measurable outcomes
> - Pilot has no scheduled go/no-go decision date
> - Leadership support is "permission to experiment" not "commitment to scale if successful"

- Project justification uses words like "innovation," "staying competitive," or "exploring use cases"

Action: Stop. Define clear business objectives and success criteria or kill the initiative. Permission to explore guarantees zombie pilot. Commitment to scale-if-successful enables real transformation.

The Human Cost

The financial waste is staggering. The human cost may be worse.

Talented data scientists become demoralized as their pilot projects languish in indefinite testing. Product managers burn out from fighting for resources to scale successful pilots while zombie projects consume budgets. Executives who know their AI strategy isn't working feel paralyzed by the magnitude of admitted waste.

This failure rate doesn't just represent lost money. It represents:

- Careers damaged by association with failed initiatives
- Talented teams trapped in projects everyone knows will fail
- Innovation budgets squandered on pilot theater instead of real transformation
- Organizational cynicism about AI's potential
- Competitive disadvantage that compounds over time

When organizations fail repeatedly at AI, they develop institutional antibodies. The next time someone proposes an AI initiative, the response is skepticism, not support. "We tried that before. It didn't work. Why would this time be different?"

This is the hidden damage: organizations aren't just wasting money—they're destroying their capacity for future transformation.

> **RED FLAG: The Zombie Pilot Epidemic**
> Your pilot is already a zombie if:
> - Running longer than 6 months without go/no-go decision
> - Success criteria have changed since launch
> - Team refers to "Phase 2 pilot" without Phase 1 decision
> - Original executive sponsor has changed or disengaged
> - No one can articulate what would trigger a kill decision
> - Metrics trending away from targets but project continues
> **Action:** Force decision within 30 days. Scale with clear production criteria, restart with new 90-day timeline and criteria, or kill and capture learnings. No fourth option.

The Path Forward

Here's the good news: the organizations that succeed at AI transformation aren't smarter, better funded, or luckier. They're more disciplined about fundamentals.

They don't chase sophisticated AI on weak foundations. They master basics first:

- Strategic clarity about business objectives before technology selection

- Leadership alignment across functions before major investment

- Internal capability building alongside vendor partnerships

- Pilot discipline that kills zombies and scales successes quickly

- Scale strategy that prepares systematically for production

- Risk management that enables innovation rather than blocking it

- Continuous evolution as systems and markets change

These aren't revolutionary insights. They're fundamentals that every successful technology transformation requires.

The difference with AI is speed and amplification. Weak foundations that might take years to collapse in traditional transformations fail in months with AI. Strong foundations that deliver incremental advantage in traditional transformations can deliver exponential advantage with AI.

AI doesn't change the fundamentals—it makes them more important.

Part II of this book presents the Seven Pillars in detail: the frameworks, assessment tools, implementation guidance, and real examples that separate the organizations that succeed from those that fail.

Part III provides the roadmap: how to assess your current state, prioritize improvements, and implement disciplines systematically.

But first, you need to understand why this keeps happening. Why do smart, experienced organizations keep making the same mistakes?

That's Chapter 2.

THE BOTTOM LINE

THE FAILURE LANDSCAPE

What Matters:

Ninety-five percent of AI initiatives fail not because of technology inadequacy but because organizations skip fundamentals: strategic clarity, leadership alignment, capability building, pilot discipline, scale strategy, risk management, and continuous evolution.

Track This:

Of your current AI initiatives, what percentage have clear business objectives (not technical goals), defined success criteria with metrics, scheduled go/no-go decisions, and internal capability being built (not just vendor dependencies)? If under 40%, you're in the 95%.

Do This:

- Within 7 days: List every AI initiative currently consuming resources

- Within 14 days: For each, document: business objective, success criteria, decision date, capability being built

- Within 30 days: Kill every initiative that can't clearly answer all four questions

Chapter Two

Why Leadership, Not Technology

Chapter 1 documented what goes wrong—the five organizational patterns that account for most of the $40 billion in annual AI waste. Strategic confusion. Vendor dependence. Zombie pilots. Capability theater. Measurement theater.

This chapter asks a harder question: why do these patterns persist in organizations led by smart, experienced people?

The answer isn't technical. It's about leadership behavior— the instincts, biases, and organizational dynamics that cause intelligent leaders to repeat the same mistakes.

The Technology Trap

The technology industry has a predictable bias: when we see challenges, we reach for technological solutions. Better tools. Faster systems. More sophisticated algorithms.

This instinct serves us well with genuinely technical problems. Performance issues? Engineer better solutions. Security vulnerabilities? Implement stronger controls.

But this instinct becomes catastrophic when applied to leadership challenges masquerading as technology problems.

When AI initiatives fail, the instinctive response is to conclude they need better AI tools, more advanced algorithms, different vendors. They chase technological solutions to what is fundamentally a leadership failure.

The research tells a different story. McKinsey identifies six foundational elements for successful digital transformation: business-led digital roadmap, talent and culture, operating model, technology, data, and adoption and scaling. Technology is one of six elements—and cannot succeed without the others. Yet most organizations pour the vast majority of resources into technology while giving lip service to the other five.

Research on AI maturity identifies four stages: Foundation (building basic knowledge), Mindset (developing AI-first thinking), Skills (honing specific capabilities), and Integration (real-time adoption). Three of four stages are entirely about people and culture, not technology.

Leadership research consistently finds that AI augments rather than replaces the human side of leadership—the communication, empathy, and collaboration that enable individuals to achieve results they couldn't achieve alone.

The pattern holds across all research: success correlates with leadership capability, not technological sophistication.

The Five Leadership Gaps

Chapter 1's five failure patterns describe symptoms. The five leadership gaps below are the underlying conditions that produce those symptoms. Strategic confusion (Pattern 1) persists because of the strategic clarity gap. Zombie pilots (Pattern 3) persist because of the pilot gap. The patterns won't stop recurring until the leadership gaps that drive them are addressed.

1. Strategic Clarity Gap

Where Chapter 1's "strategic confusion" describes organizations pursuing AI without clear objectives, the leadership gap runs deeper: leaders avoid the hard work of choosing priorities because clarity requires saying no.

Test this in your organization: Ask five executives independently to explain your AI strategy in thirty seconds. If you don't get five substantially similar answers, you have a strategic clarity gap.

Organizations with clear, communicated strategies see significantly better outcomes. Yet industry surveys suggest fewer than half have regular internal communications about AI value, and fewer than one in five establish compelling change narratives.

The gap manifests in predictable ways:

- AI pilots disconnected from business strategy

- Metrics that measure deployment rather than business impact

- Inability to prioritize when faced with multiple AI opportunities

- No clear answer to "why are we doing this?" beyond "because AI is important"

Without strategic clarity, organizations scatter resources across low-value initiatives while missing high-impact opportunities. Every AI investment becomes equally justified because no framework exists to distinguish meaningful work from distraction.

> **RED FLAG: Strategic Ambiguity**
> You have a strategic clarity gap if:
> - Your organization has more than 10 active AI pilots but cannot articulate a coherent AI strategy connecting them to business objectives
> - Different executives give conflicting explanations when asked about AI priorities
> - AI initiatives are justified by competitive pressure rather than business value
> - Success metrics focus on deployment activity rather than business outcomes
> - No framework exists for prioritizing between competing AI opportunities
>
> **Action:** Within 7 days, ask five executives independently to explain your AI strategy in 30 seconds. If answers vary significantly, convene leadership to establish clear strategic priorities and kill initiatives that don't align.

2. Alignment Gap

Senior leaders pursue conflicting priorities without effective governance to resolve tensions.

McKinsey's 2025 analysis identifies securing consensus from senior leaders on a strategy-led AI roadmap as one of the most challenging headwinds. Each business domain has distinct objectives and risk appetites. Without ongoing engagement and clear decision-making processes, AI initiatives stall in the gaps between functions.

The alignment gap shows up as:

- IT implementing AI systems without business buy-in
- Business units creating shadow AI implementations
- Finance viewing AI as cost center rather than strategic investment
- HR unprepared for workforce implications of AI adoption
- Conflicts that go unresolved until projects fail

Leadership alignment isn't a kickoff meeting. It's ongoing engagement across functions, with governance structures that resolve conflicts before they kill initiatives.

> **RED FLAG: Leadership Fragmentation**
> You have an alignment gap if:
> - Your AI governance meetings are status reports rather than decision forums
> - Conflicts get escalated rather than resolved
> - Different executives send contradictory messages about AI priorities
> - Business units are running separate, uncoordinated AI initiatives
> - Cross-functional participation is nominal rather than active
> - No clear decision-making authority exists for AI investments
>
> **Action:** Establish decision-making governance within 30 days. Define who makes which decisions, how conflicts are resolved, and what constitutes binding commitment. Kill initiatives that can't secure genuine cross-functional alignment.

3. Capability Gap

Organizations prioritize vendor contracts over internal capability building.

Industry research suggests the vast majority of the workforce will need reskilling in response to AI and automation. Yet most organizations underinvest dramatically in systematic capability building.

Research suggests that fewer than half of midlevel leaders feel their capabilities are effectively used in transformation efforts—despite being best positioned to identify practical AI applications.

The capability gap manifests as:

- Heavy reliance on external consultants and vendors

- No systematic training program for internal teams

- Loss of institutional knowledge when contractors rotate off

- Inability to maintain or adapt systems independently

- Growing vendor lock-in with decreasing negotiating leverage

Organizations that build internal capability create compound advantages—each successful initiative strengthens the organization's ability to execute the next one. Organizations that outsource expertise create compound dependencies—each new initiative requires more external support at higher cost.

RED FLAG: The Capability Void
You have a capability gap if:
- Your AI spending is 80%+ external services, 20% internal capability
- You cannot explain how your AI systems work without vendor support
- Internal teams focus on "using" platforms rather than "building" solutions

- No systematic training program exists for developing AI capabilities
- Contractor rotation causes loss of institutional knowledge
- Your negotiating leverage with vendors decreases over time

Action: Calculate your external vs. internal capability ratio. If external exceeds 3:1, immediately shift 30% of next quarter's budget to capability building. Require that every vendor engagement includes knowledge transfer and internal team development.

4. Pilot Gap

Organizations confuse pilot activity with pilot discipline.

Most organizations launch pilots readily but lack frameworks for deciding whether to scale, iterate, or kill them. McKinsey documents this pattern: organizations launch numerous pilots but few reach production because no governance exists to force go/no-go decisions.

The pilot gap appears as:

- No explicit success criteria defined before pilot launch
- Pilots that continue indefinitely without clear decision points
- "Zombie pilots" consuming resources without delivering value
- Pressure to scale pilots that haven't proven business case
- No systematic learning capture from pilot results

True pilot discipline requires clear success metrics, decision criteria defined upfront, and the courage to kill pilots that don't meet thresholds—even when politically difficult.

RED FLAG: Pilot Theater

You have a pilot discipline gap if:

- Pilots launch without explicit success criteria and decision timelines
- You have zombie pilots running longer than 6 months without go/no-go decisions
- Success criteria have changed since pilot launch
- No one has clear authority to kill failing pilots
- Political pressure prevents honest evaluation of results
- Teams refer to "Phase 2 pilot" without Phase 1 decision

Action: Within 14 days, document success criteria and decision dates for every active pilot. Force go/no-go decisions for any pilot running longer than 6 months. Kill or restart—no third option.

5. Evolution Gap

Organizations treat AI deployment as completion rather than beginning.

The compute used to train state-of-the-art AI models grows roughly four to five times per year, according to AI research tracking organizations. This pace of change means AI strategies can't follow traditional three-year planning cycles.

Yet most organizations lack mechanisms for continuous evolution. They deploy systems, declare victory, and move on. The original system gradually degrades as reality changes: business needs evolve, data patterns shift, AI capabilities advance, competitors adapt.

The evolution gap results in:

- AI strategies that become obsolete before full implementation

- Deployed systems that degrade in performance over time
- Inability to adopt new AI capabilities as they emerge
- Reactive posture to competitive moves
- No systematic learning from AI implementations

Why Leadership Matters More With AI

These five gaps exist in any technology transformation. AI amplifies their consequences in four specific ways.

AI Makes Failures More Expensive

A poorly implemented CRM costs money and frustrates users. A poorly implemented AI system can expose the organization to security vulnerabilities, create regulatory liabilities, generate biased outcomes that damage the brand, and erode workforce trust in leadership.

AI failure costs extend beyond direct financial loss to include reputational damage, regulatory risk, and organizational demoralization that undermines future transformation efforts.

AI Requires Broader Organizational Change

The widespread need for workforce reskilling confirms that AI isn't a technology project—it's an organizational transformation. This demands leadership at all levels, with particular emphasis on empowering midlevel leaders who can identify opportunities and drive adoption.

Traditional technology implementations affect specific departments. AI affects virtually every function, requiring change management capabilities most organizations haven't developed.

AI Evolves Faster Than Planning Cycles

The pace of AI advancement means strategies can't follow traditional three-year planning cycles. Compute for training state-of-the-art models continues to grow exponentially.

Organizations need continuous evolution capabilities that allow them to adapt quarterly or even monthly to new developments while maintaining strategic coherence.

AI Success Compounds

Organizations that successfully implement AI don't just solve individual problems—they build capabilities that accelerate future adoption. This compounding effect means early leadership decisions have outsized long-term consequences.

Organizations with strong foundations scale AI adoption across the enterprise. Those that accumulate bad habits find each new initiative harder than the last.

The Discipline Principle

In 2018, a pharmaceutical company launched an AI initiative to accelerate drug discovery. The science was compelling. The leadership team was experienced. The budget was adequate. Initial results looked promising.

Eighteen months later, the initiative had consumed $8 million and delivered nothing usable.

The failure wasn't technical. The AI models worked. The data infrastructure functioned. The vendor delivered everything promised.

The failure was leadership discipline—or rather, the absence of it.

The executive sponsor changed three times in eighteen months. Each brought different priorities. Strategic direction shifted from "accelerate existing research" to "identify new drug candidates" to "optimize clinical trial design"—without committing to one direction long enough to see results.

Cross-functional alignment never materialized. Research scientists viewed AI as a threat to their expertise. IT saw it as another complicated system to maintain. Finance questioned the investment without clear ROI timelines. These conflicts went unresolved because no governance structure existed to force resolution.

Capability building never happened. The organization hired expensive consultants to build models but never trained internal teams to maintain them. When consultants rotated off, institutional knowledge walked out the door.

Pilot discipline didn't exist. The initiative had no success criteria, no decision points, no learning capture. It just continued —a zombie pilot consuming resources while generating no value.

Three years later, the pattern repeated. The company hired new consultants to "fix" the AI strategy. Different vendor. Different approach. Same fundamental leadership gaps.

Same predictable outcome.

This pattern repeats across industries. The technology isn't the problem. Leadership discipline—the systematic execution of fundamentals under pressure—is what separates success from expensive failure.

The Questions That Matter

Most organizations ask the wrong questions about AI transformation:

Wrong Questions:

- Which AI technology should we use?

- How much should we invest in AI?

- Which vendor should we choose?

- How many data scientists should we hire?

- What are our competitors doing with AI?

Right Questions:

- Does our leadership team agree on why AI matters to our business strategy?

- Do we have governance structures that resolve cross-functional conflicts?

- Are we building internal capability or accumulating vendor dependencies?

- Do we have disciplined frameworks for killing pilots that aren't working?

- Can we adapt our AI strategy as technology and markets evolve?

These questions feel uncomfortable because they expose organizational weaknesses no technology purchase can fix. They demand honest assessment of leadership capability, organizational maturity, and execution discipline.

But these are the questions that predict success or failure.

From Diagnosis to Discipline

Chapter 1 showed you what the failures look like. This chapter showed you why they keep happening—the leadership behaviors that produce strategic confusion, vendor dependence, zombie pilots, capability theater, and measurement theater. The patterns are symptoms. The gaps are root causes. The Seven Pillars are the treatment protocol.

But first, we need to confront one more uncomfortable reality—the bubble dynamics driving irrational investment decisions—and develop strategies that survive regardless of whether the bubble continues inflating or begins correcting.

If your AI initiatives are failing, the technology isn't the problem.

Your leadership is.

THE BOTTOM LINE

THE LEADERSHIP GAP

What Matters:
The massive failure to generate return exists because
organizations treat AI transformation as a technology
problem requiring technology solutions. It is a leadership
problem requiring leadership solutions. Five gaps predict
failure with remarkable consistency: strategic clarity gap,
alignment gap, capability gap, pilot gap, and evolution gap.

Track This:
Ask five executives to explain your AI strategy in 30 seconds.
If you don't get five similar answers, you have a strategic
clarity gap. Count your active AI pilots—if 10+ are running
without clear kill criteria, you have a pilot discipline gap.
Calculate external vendor spending versus internal capability
investment—if ratio exceeds 3:1, you're accumulating
dependencies rather than building assets.

Do This:
- Within 7 days: Ask five executives your AI strategy test

- Within 14 days: Document success criteria and decision
dates for every active pilot

- Within 30 days: Stop launching new AI initiatives until you
can answer: (1) How does this connect to business strategy?
(2) Which executives will actively champion this? (3) What
internal capability will we build? (4) What are our go/no-go
criteria and timeline? (5) What organizational changes does
scaling require?

If you can't answer all five questions clearly, you're not ready to start—regardless of how compelling the technology seems.

Chapter Three

The Bubble Reality

Every bubble shares the same origin story: smart people get overexcited about a kernel of truth.

Every major technology transformation follows the same arc: genuine innovation creates opportunity, capital floods in, investment exceeds near-term returns, markets correct, and the underlying technology transforms industries. We've seen this with railroads, telecommunications, dot-com, and biotech.

AI is following the same trajectory.

The question for technology leaders isn't whether a correction is coming—it's how to build sustainable AI capability in an overheated market. The organizations that survive corrections aren't those that spent the most during the boom. They're those that built real capability while others accumulated expensive dependencies.

What follows examines what most AI strategy books ignore: how to position your organization to survive and thrive regardless of market dynamics.

(For current market statistics and specific indicators, see the regularly updated data supplement at whyaifails.com)

The Anatomy of Bubbles

Economist Charles Kindleberger identified five stages that characterize market bubbles across industries and eras, building on Hyman Minsky's Financial Instability Hypothesis (most fully articulated in Kindleberger's *Manias, Panics, and Crashes*, first published in 1978):

Stage 1: Displacement

A new paradigm or technology creates genuine opportunity. The innovation is real—not hype. Early adopters demonstrate clear value, attracting attention from mainstream players.

Stage 2: Boom

Early successes attract capital and attention. Investment accelerates as more players enter the market. Returns from early movers validate the opportunity, driving broader participation.

Stage 3: Euphoria

Fear of missing out drives irrational behavior. Investment decisions shift from value-based analysis to competitive positioning. Organizations invest because competitors invest, not because they have clear paths to value creation.

This pattern plays out at the company level with painful regularity. Mid-market manufacturers have committed $15 million or more to AI transformation at the peak of generative AI euphoria in 2023—without first establishing what business problem the AI would solve. The playbook is consistent: leadership announces an ambitious "AI-first" initiative, procurement signs vendor contracts under competitive urgency, and teams begin building on multiple platforms simultaneously. Each vendor promises transformative results. Each team builds proof-of-concept demos that impress in boardroom presentations.

Eighteen months later, the typical result is seven vendor contracts, four competing platforms, and zero production deployments. When the CFO demands ROI justification, leadership can't connect any initiative to a measurable business outcome. The technology worked. The vendors delivered what they promised. But no one defined what success looked like before spending began—and no one established criteria for when to stop.

This is euphoria-stage behavior at the organizational level: investment driven by fear of missing out rather than disciplined analysis of value.

Stage 4: Profit-Taking

Sophisticated investors recognize the disconnect between valuations and fundamentals. They begin exiting positions while momentum players continue entering. Volatility grows as these forces clash.

Stage 5: Panic

Markets recognize the gap between expectations and reality. Capital withdraws rapidly. Organizations that overextended face crisis; those with strong fundamentals weather the storm.

Three Components of Bubble Dynamics

AI markets currently exhibit three characteristics common to technology bubbles:

Component 1: Capital Misallocation

Infrastructure investment is outpacing demonstrated returns by historic margins. Organizations make billion-dollar commitments based on potential rather than proven value. Competitive pressure, not financial analysis, drives the spending.

The disconnect creates both opportunity—massive infrastructure buildout reduces costs and increases capability for all players—and risk. Organizations that confuse spending with capability building accumulate expensive dependencies rather than strategic assets.

Component 2: Valuation Disconnection

Market valuations reflect growth expectations rather than current financial fundamentals. Companies are valued on narrative momentum—what AI might enable—rather than demonstrated business models. This premium extends across the entire AI vendor and infrastructure stack, regardless of path to profitability.

For technology leaders, this creates both opportunity (vendors eager to prove value, negotiate partnerships) and risk (vendor consolidation or failure could disrupt dependencies).

Component 3: Capability Overpromise

The gap between demonstrated capabilities and production reality is systematically underestimated. Vendors showcase AI in controlled environments that don't reflect operational complexity. Sales cycles minimize challenges customers discover only during deployment.

This pattern is acute with generative AI: impressive demonstrations of content generation become problematic at scale, as issues around accuracy, consistency, bias, and hallucination emerge only in production.

> **RED FLAG: Bubble-Driven Decisions**
> You're making bubble-driven decisions if:
> - AI investments justified by competitive pressure rather than business value
> - Strategy documents emphasize "keeping pace" more than specific outcomes
> - Executive presentations focus on deployment speed rather than capability building
> - Board discussions ask "are we spending enough?" before "are we building assets?"
> - Vendor contracts signed without clear understanding of switching costs
>
> **Action:** Pause new AI commitments for 30 days. For each active initiative, document: (1) Business problem being solved, (2) Why AI is best solution, (3) What capability we're building internally, (4) How we'll measure success, (5) What would trigger a kill decision. Initiatives that can't answer these five aren't ready for investment.

The Pattern That Repeats

Looking across the railroad boom, electricity adoption, telecommunications buildout, dot-com bubble, and biotech speculation, a consistent pattern emerges:

Infrastructure Overinvestment Enables Transformation

Every bubble involves "wasteful" infrastructure spending that later enables genuine transformation. The railroads built too many lines too quickly—but that infrastructure powered the industrial revolution. Telecommunications companies overbuilt fiber networks in the 1990s—but that infrastructure enabled the internet economy. Current AI infrastructure investment follows the same pattern.

Early Movers Build Capability, Not Just Technology

Organizations that emerge strongest from bubbles built permanent organizational capabilities during the boom: internal expertise, proven frameworks, systematic processes. They accumulated assets, not dependencies. Organizations that only spent money emerged weaker, their "transformation" dependent on vendors and consultants who became scarce or expensive during corrections.

Corrections Separate Winners from Followers

During booms, rising markets hide poor decisions. Everyone appears to succeed. Corrections reveal who built real capability and who accumulated expensive theater.

Organizations with strong fundamentals accelerate during corrections, capturing talent and market share while competitors retreat. Organizations that overextended face crisis, scrambling to demonstrate value while budgets contract.

Strategic Patience Creates Compounding Advantage

The most successful technology adopters aren't first movers or laggards—they're disciplined fast followers who let pioneers absorb uncertainty while avoiding the paralysis of over-caution. Organizations that maintained strategic focus through bubble and correction dominated their industries. Those that chased trends or avoided commitment lost decades.

Three Strategic Postures

Organizations face three archetypal choices in bubble environments:

Posture 1: Aggressive Investment

"The risk of underinvesting exceeds the risk of overinvesting."

Some organizations make massive commitments now, arguing that capturing early advantage justifies significant capital risk. They acknowledge bubble dynamics but bet that missing the transformation poses greater danger than overinvesting.

Strategic Logic: First-mover advantages in AI—proprietary data, trained models, organizational learning—create compounding returns that justify aggressive investment even with correction risk.

Risk Profile: Overextension leaves organizations vulnerable if the correction is severe or if AI adoption doesn't meet projections. Expensive dependencies become liabilities during downturns.

Best For: Organizations with strong balance sheets, technical capability to build (not just buy), and strategic positions where early AI advantage creates defensible moats.

Posture 2: Defensive Caution

"We'll move when the technology matures and markets stabilize."

Other organizations move deliberately slowly, arguing that AI capabilities will improve while costs decrease, making it rational to wait. They see current spending as premature—paying premium prices for immature capabilities that will be better and cheaper within two to three years.

Strategic Logic: Avoiding expensive mistakes during bubble allows resources to be deployed more effectively post-correction. Waiting for consolidation, maturation, and market discipline maximizes return on investment.

Risk Profile: Competitors build capabilities that compound. By the time cautious organizations move, capability gaps may be insurmountable. Early mover advantages in AI—data network effects, organizational learning, talent attraction—accelerate over time.

Best For: Organizations in industries where AI provides incremental advantage rather than existential threat, or where being fast follower (not leader) aligns with broader strategy.

Posture 3: Strategic Capability Building

"Build organizational capability regardless of market dynamics."

The third posture focuses on accumulating permanent capabilities—internal expertise, proven frameworks, systematic processes—rather than chasing deployment speed or avoiding risk. These organizations treat bubble periods as windows to build competence that compounds through market cycles.

Strategic Logic: Organizational capability is the only truly defensible asset. Technology commoditizes, vendors consolidate, markets correct—but internal competence persists. Building capability during bubbles positions organizations to accelerate during corrections.

Risk Profile: Balanced. Neither overextending nor falling behind. Building foundations that enable future speed without incurring unsustainable debt. May appear slow during boom but proves resilient during correction.

Best For: Most organizations. This posture scales from startups to enterprises, across industries and market conditions. It's particularly effective for organizations seeking sustainable competitive advantage rather than spectacular wins or defensive positioning.

> **RED FLAG: Posture Misalignment**
> Your strategic posture is misaligned with capability if:
> - Aggressive investment posture but building vendor dependencies instead of assets
> - Defensive caution posture but competitors building insurmountable capability leads
> - Capability building posture but in practice slow deployment without learning
> - Executive messaging doesn't match resource allocation
> - Organization shifting postures based on quarterly results or market sentiment
>
> **Action:** Explicitly choose posture and align all AI decisions to it. If aggressive investment, ensure 50%+ of spending builds internal capability. If defensive caution, establish clear triggers

for when to move. If capability building, measure success by capability gained, not projects deployed. Communicate posture transparently to organization.

Five Correction-Resistant Strategies

Regardless of strategic posture, five practices build AI capability that survives market corrections:

Strategy 1: Optimize for Assets, Not Speed

The organizations that dominate post-correction aren't those that deployed fastest during the boom. They're organizations that built assets—capabilities that persist when markets shift, vendors fail, or technologies evolve.

Every AI investment should be evaluated through an asset-liability lens (formalized as a complete assessment methodology in Chapter 11): Does this build organizational capability that increases our strategic options, or does it create dependencies that constrain our future choices?

Practical Application:

- Favor solutions that transfer knowledge to internal teams
- Structure vendor contracts to build capability, not dependency
- Accept longer deployment timelines for asset-building approaches
- Measure success by capability gained, not deployment speed
- Kill initiatives that generate activity without building assets

Strategy 2: Maintain Strategic Independence

Vendor relationships are necessary. Vendor dependencies are dangerous. Strategic independence doesn't mean building everything internally—it means maintaining the capability to understand, evaluate, and if necessary rebuild what vendors provide.

Practical Application:

- Require knowledge transfer as contractual deliverable
- Build internal teams who understand vendor solutions deeply
- Maintain ability to switch vendors, however painful
- Evaluate total cost of ownership including exit costs
- Treat vendor consolidation as business continuity risk

Calculate Strategic Independence Score:

- Can you explain how systems work without vendor documentation? (25 points)
- Can you modify system behavior without vendor assistance? (25 points)
- Can you evaluate competitive offerings competently? (25 points)
- Could you rebuild core capabilities if vendor disappeared? (25 points)
- **Score below 50: High dependency risk**
- **Score 50–75: Acceptable partnership**
- **Score 75+: Strategic independence maintained**

Strategy 3: Optimize Total Cost Structure

Organizations often optimize for initial implementation cost while ignoring total cost of ownership—creating expensive surprises when licensing fees escalate, compute costs compound, or switching becomes prohibitively expensive.

Practical Application:

- Calculate 5-year total cost including vendor escalation
- Model switching costs as percentage of total investment
- Build financial models that stress-test vendor dependencies
- Evaluate fixed vs. variable costs under different scenarios

Cost Structure Resilience Test:

- What happens if vendor raises prices 30%? Usage grows 5x? Budget gets cut 40%? You need to switch vendors?
- Organizations with resilient cost structures have acceptable answers to all four

Strategy 4: Prioritize Quick Payback

During bubbles, organizations accept long payback periods—capital is cheap and patience abundant. During corrections, they demand rapid returns—capital is expensive and patience evaporates.

Correction-resistant strategies prioritize initiatives with clear paths to value within 12–18 months, regardless of market conditions. This discipline prevents accumulating expensive pilots that never generate returns.

Practical Application:

* Favor initiatives targeting high-cost problems with clear
  savings
* Require business case with payback period < 18 months
* Kill initiatives that can't demonstrate path to value
* Celebrate early returns (even modest ones)
* Use quick wins to fund longer-term capability building

Quick payback doesn't mean short-term thinking. Early returns build credibility for strategic investments, creating a virtuous cycle: returns fund capability building; capability accelerates returns.

Strategy 5: Build Internal Capability Strength

External dependencies—on consultants, vendors, contractors—create vulnerability during corrections. Organizations with strong internal capabilities sustain momentum through market volatility.

Practical Application:

* Hire for capability building, not just deployment
* Invest in systematic training and development
* Use consultants to transfer knowledge, not just deliver
  projects
* Build communities of practice internally
* Measure success by capability gained, not projects
  completed
* Create career paths that retain expertise

Capability Building Metrics:

- Percentage of AI work performed by internal teams (target: 60%+)

- Knowledge transfer score from vendor engagements (target: 80%+)

- Internal teams' ability to execute without external support (target: 75%+)

- Retention rate of AI talent (target: 90%+)

- Speed improvement on successive initiatives (target: 30% faster each time)

RED FLAG: Correction Vulnerability
Your organization is vulnerable to market correction if:
- Most AI spending creates vendor dependencies rather than internal capability
- Average initiative payback period exceeds 24 months
- Total cost of ownership grows faster than value delivered
- Strategic independence score below 50 (see Strategy 2)
- External resources (consultants, contractors) exceed 60% of AI team capacity
- No one can articulate what happens if top 3 vendors raise prices 30%

Action: Conduct correction stress test. Model scenarios: (1) Vendor prices increase 30%, (2) AI budget cut 40%, (3) Top vendor exits market, (4) Key consultants unavailable. For each scenario, document: What breaks? What's at risk? What's our response? If answers are "everything breaks" and "we don't know," you're overextended. Begin building strategic independence immediately.

Positioning for Post-Correction Advantage

Correction timing is unpredictable. But organizations can position to capitalize regardless of when it occurs:

Opportunity 1: Talent Acquisition

Market corrections invert talent dynamics. Competition for AI talent decreases. Compensation expectations moderate. Strong organizations acquire capabilities that were unaffordable or unavailable during boom periods.

But only if they built the internal capability to attract, deploy, and retain that talent effectively. Organizations without established AI programs struggle to attract talent even when markets soften.

Opportunity 2: Capability Acquisition

Vendor consolidation creates opportunities to acquire technologies, platforms, and capabilities at favorable terms. Organizations with strong balance sheets and clear strategies build through acquisition what would have been expensive or slow to develop organically.

But only if they maintained financial discipline during the boom. Organizations that overspent during euphoria lack resources when acquisition opportunities emerge.

Opportunity 3: Market Share Capture

Competitors who overextended or stayed excessively cautious face constraints. Organizations that built sustainable capability extend market leadership while others retreat or struggle to catch up.

The most significant competitive advantages emerge during corrections, not booms. But only for organizations positioned to maintain investment while competitors pull back.

This dynamic has played out in energy companies that maintained strategic discipline during the 2023–2024 AI spending surge. Rather than chasing generative AI headlines, these organizations focused on three operational AI applications tied to specific cost problems: predictive equipment maintenance that reduced unplanned downtime, energy demand forecasting that optimized purchasing, and supply chain optimization that cut carrying costs. Each initiative had a defined business case, measurable targets, and a ninety-day decision gate. While competitors signed enterprise agreements with generative AI vendors promising transformation, these disciplined organizations built narrowly scoped production systems that delivered measurable value within twelve months.

When competitors began pulling back spending in late 2024 —boards suddenly demanding ROI justification for generative AI experiments—the disciplined companies had three systems in production generating documented savings. They acquired AI talent from overstaffed competitors at reasonable rates, expanding capability precisely when the market made it affordable. They turned a correction into an acceleration—not through luck, but through the strategic patience that correction-resistant capability demands.

Opportunity 4: Economic Reset and Thought Leadership

Vendor pricing, partnership terms, and platform costs typically reset during corrections. Organizations with strategic independence can renegotiate at favorable terms—but only if they avoided deep dependencies during the boom. Simultaneously, market uncertainty creates space for disciplined organizations to establish themselves as voices of reason, building lasting brand value and competitive position.

The Governance Shift

Bubble environments reward aggressive deployment. Correction environments reward disciplined value creation. Organizations need governance systems that shift between modes without losing strategic coherence.

During Bubble Periods: Lower approval thresholds to enable experimentation. Accept learning value alongside business value. Encourage portfolio breadth. Support strategic pilot failures as part of learning.

During Correction Periods: Raise approval thresholds to ensure value focus. Concentrate portfolio around proven winners. Eliminate initiatives that can't demonstrate clear path to value. Celebrate efficiency and return on investment.

The key is governance that adjusts to market conditions while maintaining strategic consistency. Establish trigger points—market indicators (valuation multiples, investment flows), internal indicators (budget pressure, ROI scrutiny), and competitive indicators (peer behavior, market positioning). When triggers activate, adjust systematically: communicate rationale transparently, maintain strategic continuity while shifting tactics, and accelerate proven initiatives while pausing exploratory ones.

The Contrarian Advantage

The organizations that emerge strongest from technology transformations adopt contrarian positions during volatile periods. When others panic and retrench, they maintain strategic AI investment, capture talent, and extend market leadership. When others chase aggressive deployment, they focus on sustainable capability building, maintain financial discipline, and let pioneers absorb uncertainty while learning from their mistakes.

The contrarian position isn't about being different for its own sake—it's about maintaining strategic discipline when market sentiment drives emotional reactions.

What History Teaches

In 2000, the dot-com bubble burst. Organizations that had spent millions on digital initiatives faced brutal scrutiny. Many abandoned web strategies entirely, declaring the internet "overhyped."

Twenty years later, the organizations that maintained strategic focus on digital capability—even through the correction—dominated their industries. Those that pulled back lost a decade.

In 2008, the financial crisis forced severe budget cuts across industries. Organizations slashed innovation spending, including nascent mobile and cloud initiatives. The correction seemed to validate caution.

Fifteen years later, the organizations that maintained strategic investment in mobile and cloud—even through crisis—had built insurmountable leads. Those that retreated faced expensive catch-up campaigns.

AI will follow the same pattern. Current market dynamics will correct. Some organizations will overreact, abandoning AI as "overhyped" or "not ready." Others will maintain discipline and keep building capability.

Five years from now, the winners won't be those who spent the most during the bubble. They'll be organizations that:

- Built real capability rather than vendor dependency
- Maintained discipline during bubble and correction
- Focused on fundamentals regardless of market sentiment
- Continued strategic investment while competitors panicked
- Emerged from correction stronger, not weaker

The Ultimate Truth:

Corrections are temporary. Capability is permanent.

Organizations that maintain discipline through bubbles and corrections build durable competitive advantage. The rest chase trends and overreact to volatility.

The rest of this book provides the framework for building that permanent capability: the Seven Pillars of AI leadership that enable success regardless of market conditions, technology generations, or organizational changes.

But first, we need to understand what strategic clarity means in practice—and why so few organizations achieve it.

> **RED FLAG: The Vendor Lock-In Trap**
>
> You're building vendor dependencies, not capabilities, if:
>
> - More than 60% of AI work is done by external vendors/consultants
>
> - You can't explain how your AI systems work without vendor documentation
>
> - Internal team focuses on "using" platforms rather than "building" solutions
>
> - Vendor contracts include automatic price escalation clauses
>
> - You haven't evaluated what internal development would cost versus ongoing vendor fees
>
> **Action:** Calculate true total cost of ownership over 5 years including vendor dependencies. If migration cost exceeds 2x original implementation, you're locked in. Build exit strategy now.

THE BOTTOM LINE

THE BUBBLE REALITY

What Matters:
Every technology transformation follows predictable bubble
dynamics. AI is no exception. Organizations that build
correction-resistant capability—focusing on assets over speed,
maintaining strategic independence, optimizing total cost
structure, prioritizing quick payback, and building internal
strength—survive and thrive regardless of market conditions.

Track This:
Calculate your Strategic Independence Score (Strategy 2).
Model what happens if: (1) top vendors raise prices 30%, (2) AI
budget cut 40%, (3) key vendor exits market. If answers
suggest high vulnerability, you're overextended. Measure
what percentage of AI spending builds internal capability vs.
vendor dependency—target 60%+ internal.

Do This:
- Within 7 days: Choose explicit strategic posture (aggressive,
cautious, or capability-building) and align all decisions to it

- Within 14 days: Conduct correction stress test on current AI
portfolio

- Within 30 days: For each active initiative, document:
business problem, internal capability being built, 5-year total
cost, strategic independence score, payback period. Kill
initiatives that fail multiple tests.

Corrections are temporary. Capability is permanent. The
organizations that dominate post-correction aren't those

spending most now—they're those building sustainable capability while others accumulate dependencies.

PART II: THE SEVEN PILLARS

Chapter Four

Strategic Clarity—The North Star Principle

A regional bank was losing commercial lending deals to online lenders who could approve credit in hours, not weeks. Their fourteen-day credit decision cycle was bleeding market share. The turning point came in a strategy session—the CEO stood at a whiteboard, crossed out a page of bullet points, and wrote a single sentence: "Reduce credit decision cycle time from fourteen days to twenty-four hours while maintaining current loss rates."

That sentence changed everything. Every proposed AI initiative faced one test: Does this accelerate credit decisions? Does it maintain acceptable risk? If not, they didn't pursue it—regardless of how innovative or interesting it seemed. Over eighteen months, they went from seventeen scattered pilots to three focused initiatives, all connected to that North Star. All three reached production. Combined first-year value: $6.8 million against $2.1 million in investment.

Most organizations never achieve this clarity. Research across dozens of Fortune 500 organizations reveals that remarkably few can pass this test consistently. The rest had AI strategies that read like vendor brochures—initiatives aimed at "exploring AI capabilities" or "building innovation culture," executives who could spend twenty minutes explaining their AI approach without once mentioning a specific business outcome they intended to achieve.

Strategic clarity isn't about sophisticated analysis. It's about answering basic questions honestly: What problem are we solving? Why does solving it matter? How will we know if we've succeeded? What are we explicitly choosing not to do?

The Cost of Strategic Ambiguity

Organizations with clearly articulated AI strategies are consistently more likely to achieve their objectives than those pursuing what practitioners call "technology-first" or "opportunistic" approaches. The pattern is stark: clarity predicts success with remarkable consistency.

Yet strategic ambiguity remains the norm. Consider these actual strategy statements from major enterprises:

"Leverage AI to drive innovation and competitive advantage across our business."

"Explore AI capabilities to enhance customer experience and operational efficiency."

"Become an AI-powered organization that leads our industry in digital transformation."

These aren't strategies. They're aspirations wrapped in buzzwords—statements so vague they could apply to any organization in any industry. They create no boundaries, establish no priorities, and enable no meaningful decisions. When everything is strategic, nothing is.

The damage compounds fast. Without strategic clarity, organizations can't distinguish valuable initiatives from theater. They can't allocate resources rationally or establish meaningful success criteria. They can't build coalitions around shared objectives or make intelligent trade-offs between competing investments.

Most critically, they can't fail deliberately. When strategy is ambiguous, every initiative can claim alignment. Projects that should die early persist indefinitely, consuming resources while delivering nothing—the zombie pilots that Chapter 7's Pilot Discipline framework directly addresses.

Strategic ambiguity breeds what I call "defensive decision-making"—leaders avoiding difficult choices by maintaining deliberately vague objectives that let all stakeholders claim victory. Politically safe in the short term. Strategically fatal over time.

The North Star Principle

Strategic clarity starts with what I call the North Star Principle: every AI investment must orient toward a single, clearly articulated strategic objective that connects technology to business value. Not five objectives. Not a balanced scorecard. One dominant purpose that everyone—from the CEO to the newest engineer—can explain in a single sentence.

This makes executives uncomfortable. They worry about oversimplification, about missing opportunities, about appearing narrow-minded. They want comprehensive strategies that address multiple stakeholders and demonstrate sophisticated thinking.

But comprehensiveness and clarity are enemies. The more objectives your strategy tries to serve, the less guidance it provides. A strategy that must satisfy everyone ends up directing no one.

Consider a financial services organization in 2023. Their AI strategy listed twelve strategic objectives, from "enhance customer experience" to "improve regulatory compliance" to "drive operational efficiency." Every stakeholder saw their priorities reflected. Every initiative could claim alignment.

The result? Seventeen simultaneous pilots with no coherent connection to each other or to actual business priorities. Customer experience teams built chatbots while risk teams built fraud detection while operations teams built document processing—all claiming alignment, none aware of the others' work, and no one responsible for ensuring any of it created value.

When pressed to identify their single most important AI objective, the executive team couldn't reach consensus. They had a strategy that comforted everyone and directed no one.

Compare this to the regional bank from this chapter's opening. Their North Star—"reduce credit decision cycle time from fourteen days to twenty-four hours while maintaining current loss rates"—was one sentence. Measurable. Connected to competitive advantage. Every proposed initiative faced that test. Three focused initiatives survived: document intelligence for loan applications, automated income verification, and real-time credit risk modeling.

The difference wasn't technical sophistication. It was strategic discipline. They knew what they were building and why. They could evaluate every decision against a clear standard. They could say no.

The Five Strategic Questions

Strategic clarity isn't mysterious. It emerges from honest answers to five fundamental questions. Organizations that succeed answer these questions explicitly and revisit them quarterly. Most either never answer them at all or answer them so vaguely that the answers provide no guidance.

The Five Strategic Questions radiate from a central North Star—your organization's core strategic purpose. Question 1 (Why are we investing in AI?) establishes the foundation. Questions 2 and 4 define the boundaries—what capabilities AI will enable and what you are explicitly choosing not to do. Question 3 extends the timeline to a three-year vision. Question 5 closes the loop with measurable success criteria. Together, they form a decision framework that every initiative must pass through.

Question 1: Why Are We Investing in AI?

Not "to drive innovation" or "to stay competitive." Those aren't answers—they're substitutes for thinking. The question demands specificity: What business problem does AI solve better than any alternative? What opportunity does it create that justifies the investment and risk?

Across industries, organizations that begin with clearly articulated business problems are far more likely to achieve measurable returns than those starting with technology exploration. The causality runs one direction: problem clarity enables solution success.

Yet many organizations reverse this. They start with AI capabilities and search for problems to apply them to. This is why vendor demonstrations spawn so many pilots—the technology looks impressive, someone identifies a plausible use case, and an initiative launches without ever establishing why solving this particular problem matters more than the hundred other problems the organization faces.

The discipline required: Complete this sentence in twenty words or less. "We're investing in AI because solving [specific problem] would [specific business outcome] which would [measurable value]."

If you can't complete that sentence, you're not ready to invest.

Question 2: What Specific Capabilities Will AI Enable?

Not "we'll use machine learning" or "we'll apply natural language processing." Those describe technologies, not capabilities. The question asks: What will your organization do after this investment that it cannot do today? How will those capabilities create competitive advantage?

A clear pattern emerges across industries: organizations that define AI investments in terms of capabilities ("make credit decisions in real-time," "detect quality defects at line speed") reach production deployment at significantly higher rates than those defining investments in terms of technologies ("implement deep learning," "deploy large language models").

The distinction matters because capabilities connect to business value; technologies don't. Technologies become obsolete. Capabilities compound. An organization that builds real-time credit decision capability can apply that advantage across products and geographies. An organization that merely installed a particular machine learning model owns a depreciating asset requiring continuous investment to maintain.

Consider two manufacturing organizations pursuing AI for quality control. The first frames their objective as "implement computer vision for defect detection." The second frames theirs as "achieve real-time quality feedback at every production stage." Both use similar technology. One is building a capability. The other is installing a tool.

Three years later, the capability-focused organization has extended its quality system across twelve production lines and three facilities. The technology-focused organization is still debugging its initial installation and debating whether to upgrade to newer vision systems.

The capability framework created compound advantages. The technology framework created maintenance obligations.

Question 3: What's Our Three-Year Vision?

AI transformation doesn't happen in quarters. Capability building requires sustained investment over multiple years. Organizations need a vision substantial enough to justify that investment—not a specific roadmap (those become obsolete) but a clear picture of the capabilities they're building and the competitive advantages those capabilities will create.

Organizational transformation research shows that initiatives with multi-year strategic horizons but annual adjustment cycles achieve substantially higher success rates than either short-term tactical approaches or rigid long-term plans.

The three-year timeframe forces executives to think beyond immediate pilots while staying concrete enough to drive decisions. Long enough to build real capability. Short enough to maintain accountability.

The test: Can your executive team describe, without referencing specific technologies, what your organization will be capable of doing in three years that it cannot do today? Can they explain why those capabilities will create competitive advantage? Can they estimate the business value those capabilities will generate?

If answers vary significantly across executives, you don't have a vision. You have individual interpretations of ambiguous intentions.

Question 4: What Are We Explicitly Not Doing?

This is the hardest question because it demands saying no. Every AI opportunity looks interesting. Every use case someone proposes has merit. But organizations have finite resources, finite attention, and finite capacity to build capability. Strategy is as much about what you won't do as what you will.

The discipline: Name three significant AI opportunities you've explicitly rejected in the past six months. If you can't, you're not making strategic choices—you're accumulating initiatives until resource constraints force triage.

Great strategies create clarity through exclusion. They establish boundaries that make prioritization possible. They enable teams to evaluate new opportunities against explicit criteria rather than subjective enthusiasm.

The regional bank mentioned earlier maintained a "not doing" list: no AI for marketing optimization, no AI for HR processes, no AI for facilities management. All potentially valuable. All explicitly excluded because they didn't advance the North Star of faster credit decisions.

When new opportunities arose—and they always do—the leadership team had a clear framework for evaluation. Does this accelerate credit decisions? No? Then it's in the "not doing" category regardless of how interesting it might be.

This enabled focus. It also enabled trust. Teams knew that rejected initiatives weren't political casualties or oversight—they were strategic choices. Leadership wasn't saying "not yet" or "maybe later." They were saying "no, because it doesn't advance our strategy."

Question 5: How Will We Know We're Succeeding?

Vague metrics enable vague accountability. "Improve customer experience" sounds strategic until you realize no one can measure it meaningfully—which means no one can manage or evaluate it. Strategic clarity requires specific success metrics established upfront—not activities (pilots launched, models deployed) but business outcomes (revenue increased, costs reduced, risks mitigated).

Across multiple industries, organizations with clearly defined success metrics achieve their AI objectives at dramatically higher rates than those measuring "progress" through activity-based proxies.

The pattern among successful organizations: they define success in business terms first, then translate to technical metrics. Failed organizations do the reverse—they celebrate technical achievements (model accuracy improved! processing speed increased!) without ever connecting those achievements to business value.

The discipline: Complete these sentences before any significant AI investment:

- "We will know we've succeeded when [specific business metric] reaches [specific target] by [specific date]."

- "If we achieve only [minimum acceptable result], we will [specific action—kill it, continue it, or scale it]."

- "We will measure success by [business outcome metric], not by [technical metric]."

The requirement for minimums is critical. It forces organizations to establish kill criteria—the point at which continued investment becomes irrational regardless of sunk costs or political pressure. Without predetermined kill criteria, initiatives become zombies: technically alive but delivering no value, consuming resources that could produce better returns elsewhere.

Three Failure Patterns

Strategic clarity fails in predictable ways. No organization intends to pursue vague strategies or let initiatives drift indefinitely. They fall into failure through patterns that seem reasonable in the moment but prove toxic over time.

Failure Pattern 1: The Buffet Strategy

This is the "try everything" approach: simultaneous initiatives across multiple domains with no coherent connection between them. Leadership approves anything that seems interesting or innovative, creating a portfolio that resembles a buffet—a little of this, a little of that, nothing pursued with sufficient focus to succeed.

The buffet strategy grows from good intentions. Executives worry about missing opportunities. They want to "explore AI's potential." They believe that more experiments increase the probability that something will work.

But this logic ignores capacity constraints. No organization can build capability in twelve directions simultaneously, maintain focus across seventeen pilots, or develop expertise in every AI technology and application domain. The buffet strategy guarantees superficial capability across many areas and deep capability in none.

The pattern is clear: organizations running fewer concurrent AI initiatives are significantly more likely to reach production deployment than those running ten or more simultaneous experiments. Focus compounds. Fragmentation dissipates.

> **RED FLAG: The Buffet Syndrome**
> You have a buffet strategy if:
> - You're running more than ten AI initiatives without clear strategic coherence
> - New initiatives get approved because they're "interesting" rather than strategic
> - No one can explain how current portfolio connects to a single strategic objective
> - Teams compete for resources rather than collaborating toward shared goals
> - Portfolio reviews focus on individual project status rather than strategic alignment
>
> **Action:** List every active AI initiative. For each, require a one-sentence connection to your North Star strategic objective. Initiatives that can't connect get killed or paused within 30 days. Reduce concurrent initiatives to five or fewer until strategic clarity is established.

Failure Pattern 2: The Zombie Strategy

This pattern preserves initiatives long past the point where rational evaluation would terminate them. Pilots that should have reached go/no-go decisions months ago keep running. Experiments that failed to meet success criteria morph into "Phase 2" with adjusted goals. Projects that should die instead request additional time and resources.

Zombie strategies emerge because organizations set vague success criteria (or none at all), making it politically difficult to kill failed initiatives. Without predetermined kill criteria, termination requires someone to publicly declare failure—and in politically sensitive environments, continuing to fund the zombie becomes easier than pulling the plug.

The damage accumulates. Resources consumed by zombies can't fund better opportunities. Teams working on failing initiatives grow demoralized. The organization develops a reputation for dodging hard decisions, which breeds more zombie-producing behavior.

The antidote: predetermined kill criteria established before initiatives begin. Define minimum success thresholds. Specify decision timelines. Assign decision authority to someone with both the incentive and the power to kill failures.

The regional bank's discipline was instructive. Every pilot had a six-month limit and predetermined success criteria. At month six, one of three decisions: kill it, iterate for three more months with adjusted goals, or move to production. No exceptions, no delays, no "Phase 2" deferrals.

This discipline killed seven of their seventeen original pilots. Those kills freed resources that funded the three initiatives that ultimately succeeded. Without the discipline to kill zombies, they would have continued funding marginal experiments indefinitely while under-resourcing the initiatives that actually worked.

> **RED FLAG: Buzzword Strategy**
> Your strategy is theater if:
> - It uses "AI-powered," "leverage," or "transform" more than specific verbs describing what you'll actually do differently
> - Strategy could apply to any company in any industry without modification

- Board presentations focus on technology capabilities rather than business outcomes
- Success stories highlight deployment activity ("launched 15 pilots") rather than value delivered
- No one has been fired or reassigned based on strategic performance

Action: Ban buzzwords from your next strategy review. Require every statement to include: specific business problem, measurable outcome, and timeline. If the strategy can't survive this filter, start over with the Five Strategic Questions.

Failure Pattern 3: Vague Aspiration

This is the "we want to be an AI-powered organization" strategy—high-level aspirations with no specific objectives, no clear priorities, no defined path from current state to desired state. These strategies sound polished in board presentations. They provide no guidance for actual decision-making.

Vague aspiration strategies emerge when executives feel pressure to "have an AI strategy" but haven't invested the time to develop real clarity. They hire consultants who deliver polished slide decks. They announce AI initiatives in earnings calls. They establish AI centers of excellence.

But when individual teams ask "what should we actually do?" the strategy provides no answers. So teams improvise. They attend vendor conferences and launch pilots based on demonstrations. They pursue whatever seems interesting or achievable. Strategic theater replaces strategic clarity.

Failed transformations show the same pattern repeatedly: vague strategic aspirations correlate with organizational confusion, duplicated efforts, and eventual initiative abandonment.

The antidote is forcing specificity. Don't accept strategies that any organization in any industry could deliver. Demand answers that connect AI capabilities to specific business problems whose solutions would create measurable competitive advantage.

If you can present your AI strategy without mentioning your industry, customers, or specific business challenges, you have vague aspiration, not strategic clarity.

> **RED FLAG: The Vendor Roadmap Trap**
> You've outsourced strategic thinking if:
> - Your strategy mentions vendor platform capabilities more than customer problems
> - AI roadmap mirrors vendor product roadmap rather than business priorities
> - Technology selection preceded problem definition
> - Vendor demonstrations drive initiative launches more than business cases
> - Strategic planning sessions include vendors but not front-line business leaders
>
> **Action:** Review your current AI strategy document. Count vendor/technology references versus business problem references. If technology references exceed 2:1, rewrite starting from business problems. Ban vendor names from strategy documents—focus on capabilities needed, not products selected.

The Strategy Statement

Strategic clarity requires documentation—not extensive plans or elaborate roadmaps, but a clear statement of strategic intent that anyone in the organization can understand and use to evaluate decisions. I use a template that forces the specificity strategic clarity demands:

STRATEGY STATEMENT TEMPLATE

Our AI Strategic Objective:

[One sentence describing the dominant business objective AI will enable]

Business Problem We're Solving:

[2-3 sentences describing the specific problem and why solving it matters]

Capabilities We're Building:

[Bullet list of 3-5 specific capabilities, each connected to business value]

Success Metrics:

[Specific, measurable outcomes with targets and timelines]

What We're Not Doing:

[Explicit exclusions—opportunities we're choosing not to pursue]

Strategic Dependencies:

[What must be true for this strategy to succeed—capabilities, partnerships, resources]

The entire statement should fit on a single page. If it requires more, you're not being strategic—you're being comprehensive. Comprehensiveness and clarity are enemies.

The regional bank's strategy statement ran 487 words. One page. Anyone in the organization could read it in ninety seconds and understand exactly what they were building and why. Compare that to the seventeen-page strategy document from the financial services organization with twelve objectives—impressive to review, impossible to use for decision-making.

The power isn't in the template. It's in the discipline the template enforces: specificity over comprehensiveness, clarity over sophistication, guidance over impressiveness.

Strategic Clarity Assessment

The disciplined minority assess their strategic clarity regularly using structured frameworks. They don't wait for failure signals—they proactively evaluate whether their strategy provides sufficient guidance for decision-making and sufficient focus for capability building.

I use a six-dimension assessment framework:

1. Articulation Clarity (5 questions)

- Can executives explain the strategy in under ninety seconds without slides?
- Do explanations from different executives align?
- Can teams connect their work to strategic objectives?
- Is the strategy specific to your organization and industry?
- Does the strategy force meaningful trade-offs?

2. Metric Clarity (5 questions)

- Are success metrics defined in business terms, not technical terms?
- Are targets specific and time-bound?
- Are minimum success thresholds established?
- Can progress be measured at least quarterly?

- Do metrics focus on outcomes, not activities?

3. Scope Clarity (5 questions)

- Are strategic boundaries clearly defined?
- Can teams easily determine if proposed initiatives align to
    strategy?
- Are explicit exclusions documented?
- Is the number of concurrent initiatives manageable?
- Does portfolio composition reflect strategic priorities?

4. Decision Clarity (5 questions)

- Does strategy enable go/no-go decisions on pilots?
- Are kill criteria predetermined before initiatives begin?
- Can resource allocation be justified by strategic priorities?
- Are trade-off decisions made explicitly against strategy?
- Can initiatives be terminated based on strategic criteria?

5. Communication Clarity (5 questions)

- Is strategy documented in accessible form?
- Have all stakeholders been briefed on strategy?
- Do teams reference strategy in planning and reviews?
- Are new initiatives evaluated against strategic criteria?
- Is strategy reinforced in executive communications?

6. Maintenance Clarity (5 questions)

- Is strategy reviewed quarterly?
- Are strategic adjustments made deliberately, not
    reactively?

- Does portfolio composition get adjusted to maintain strategic focus?

- Are teams held accountable to strategic objectives?

- Is strategic discipline reinforced through governance?

Scoring: Each question scored 0 (no) or 1 (yes)

- 26–30: Excellent strategic clarity

- 21–25: Good clarity, minor gaps

- 16–20: Moderate clarity, needs strengthening

- 11–15: Weak clarity, urgent improvement needed

- <11: No strategic clarity, fundamental problem

Most organizations score in the 11–15 range—weak clarity that explains why their initiatives struggle. Organizations that succeed consistently score above 25.

The assessment isn't academic. It's diagnostic. Low scores in specific dimensions reveal where clarity breaks down and what needs strengthening.

[Digital Resource: Complete 30-question Strategic Clarity Assessment available at whyaifails.com]

Maintaining Strategic Clarity

Strategic clarity isn't established once and maintained forever. Market conditions change. Technologies evolve. Organizational priorities shift. Strategy must adapt—but adaptation doesn't mean constant revision. Organizations that rewrite strategy quarterly based on the latest trends create confusion, not clarity.

The discipline: review strategy quarterly, revise strategy rarely. Four maintenance practices sustain strategic clarity:

Practice 1: Quarterly Strategy Reviews

Review (don't revise) strategy every quarter. Ask:

- Does strategy still connect to business priorities?
- Are initiatives aligned to strategic objectives?
- Do success metrics still measure what matters?
- Are resources allocated according to strategic priorities?
- Should any initiatives be killed based on strategic criteria?

Most quarters, the answer is "strategy remains valid, continue execution." The review identifies drift before it becomes crisis.

Practice 2: Annual Strategy Refresh

Once per year, conduct deeper strategic assessment:

- Have market conditions changed sufficiently to require strategic adjustment?
- Are competitive dynamics different than assumed?
- Have organizational priorities shifted?
- Is the strategy still distinctive and defensible?
- Are capabilities building as anticipated?

This is where strategic pivots happen—but pivots should be rare (every two to three years) and deliberate, not quarterly reactions to trends.

Practice 3: Initiative-Strategy Mapping

Maintain explicit mapping of every AI initiative to strategic objectives. This isn't bureaucracy—it's clarity maintenance. The mapping reveals portfolio drift: initiatives accumulate that don't connect to strategy, resources flow to non-strategic activities, or strategic priorities starve for investment.

The discipline: before approving any new initiative, require explicit connection to documented strategic objectives. If connection can't be made, don't approve—regardless of how interesting or innovative the opportunity seems.

Practice 4: Kill Non-Strategic Initiatives

Periodically audit your portfolio and terminate initiatives that don't connect to strategic objectives—even technically successful ones. This is extraordinarily difficult politically. Teams will argue that their work has merit. They'll request exceptions or propose adjusted objectives.

The discipline: strategic alignment isn't optional. Initiatives that don't advance strategic objectives, regardless of technical success, consume resources better deployed elsewhere. Kill them.

The regional bank killed three technically successful pilots because they didn't advance the North Star of faster credit decisions. The capabilities those pilots developed were impressive. They also weren't strategic. Killing them freed resources that funded expansion of the initiatives that were.

That's strategic discipline. It takes courage because every terminated initiative creates disappointed stakeholders. But the alternative—maintaining initiatives because they're interesting rather than strategic—dissipates focus and guarantees mediocrity.

The Clarity Imperative

Strategic clarity isn't complicated. It's disciplined. It demands answering basic questions honestly and acting on those answers —saying no to interesting opportunities that don't advance strategy, killing initiatives that fail to meet predetermined criteria, maintaining focus despite constant pressure to chase every promising possibility.

Most organizations never establish real clarity. They pursue vague strategies that let every stakeholder see their priorities reflected but provide no guidance for decision-making. They accumulate initiatives like buffet diners accumulate plates—a little of everything, satisfaction from nothing.

The rare few who translate AI investment into competitive advantage establish one clear North Star. They answer the five strategic questions explicitly. They document their strategy concisely. They maintain discipline quarterly. They build coalition around clear objectives rather than vague aspirations.

They succeed not because they're more sophisticated but because they're more disciplined. They know what they're building and why. They can evaluate every decision against clear criteria. They can say no.

Strategy isn't what you write in PowerPoint decks. It's what you do when forced to choose between competing opportunities. Organizations with clarity make those choices deliberately, based on predetermined criteria. Organizations without clarity make them reactively—based on whoever shouts loudest or whatever seems most interesting this quarter.

You either solve the problem or you don't. Sophistication doesn't substitute for focus. Comprehensiveness doesn't substitute for clarity. Innovation theater doesn't substitute for strategic discipline.

THE BOTTOM LINE

THE NORTH STAR PRINCIPLE

What Matters:
Strategic clarity separates organizations that succeed from those that waste billions chasing technology without purpose. One clearly articulated North Star objective—not five, not twelve—provides the decision framework that prevents zombie pilots, eliminates buffet strategies, and focuses resources on initiatives that create measurable value.

Track This:
Percentage of AI initiatives directly tied to documented strategic objectives with clear success metrics (target: 90%+). Number of concurrent initiatives (target: five or fewer). Strategic Clarity Assessment score (target: 25+ out of 30).

Do This:
- Within 7 days: Complete the Strategy Statement Template—one page, one North Star objective

- Within 14 days: Map every active AI initiative to that objective; flag any that can't connect

- Within 30 days: Kill or pause initiatives that don't advance the North Star, and require a 60-second strategy explanation from every executive on your leadership team

Strategic clarity is the foundation. Without it, every other pillar crumbles under the weight of competing agendas and vendor roadmaps.

Clarity without coalition is just well-documented failure. The next pillar, Leadership Alignment, is where we turn next.

Chapter Five

Leadership Alignment— Building the Coalition

Six months into a major AI transformation, the CIO received an urgent call from the VP of Sales. "We need to talk about this AI project. It's not working."

It was a confusing message. The initiative in question—using machine learning (ML) to prioritize sales leads—had exceeded every technical performance goal. The model was accurate, the system was reliable, and early users reported strong results.

"What's not working?" the CIO asked.

"Nobody's using it," he replied. "My team doesn't trust it. They think it's going to replace them. And honestly, I'm not sure I pushed it hard enough because I'm not convinced either."

This conversation exposed a critical strategic error. They had the right technology solving the right problem with the right metrics. But they lacked the coalition of leaders necessary to drive adoption. The sales VP wasn't aligned, his managers weren't committed, and the frontline salespeople felt threatened rather than empowered.

Leadership alignment—the second pillar—addresses this gap. Changing how people work, what they prioritize, and how they measure success cannot be mandated from the CIO's office. It requires a coalition of leaders across the organization who understand the strategy, believe in the approach, and actively champion the effort.

The Alignment Gap

Here's what typically happens in AI transformations:

What IT Thinks: "We're building a tool that will help the business work more effectively. Once it's ready, people will use it because it makes their jobs easier."

What Business Leaders Think: "IT is doing another technology project. I'll let them know what we need, but honestly, I have more pressing priorities. I'll check in when it's ready to deploy."

What Employees Think: "They're building an AI system that will probably take our jobs or at least change our roles in ways we don't want. Nobody asked us what we actually need."

This alignment gap—the distance between what different groups think is happening—determines whether transformation succeeds or stalls. It emerges because stakeholders hold different information, incentives, authority, risk tolerance, and time horizons. Bridging it requires deliberate, sustained effort to build shared understanding and commitment across leadership.

Most technology leaders underinvest in coalition building because it feels like politics rather than progress. Technical work is more comfortable than stakeholder management. Results aren't visible the way code or deployments are. It demands vulnerability in acknowledging concerns. It forces trade-offs between stakeholder preferences.

But here's the reality: you can build perfect AI systems that no one uses. You can solve important problems that no one values. You can demonstrate impressive results that no one acts on. Leadership alignment is the difference between AI as science project and AI as business transformation.

The Coalition Building Framework

Effective coalitions don't form by accident. They require systematic work: identifying stakeholders, understanding their perspectives, addressing concerns, and securing commitment.

Phase 1: Stakeholder Mapping

Identify everyone whose support or resistance materially affects success. For each stakeholder, document their role and authority, current alignment level (champion, supporter, neutral, skeptic, or resistor), key concerns, and influence pattern.

Your stakeholder map should answer three critical questions:

1. **Who can kill this initiative?** Identify blockers and veto holders—stakeholders who can unilaterally stop progress. These require the most careful management.

2. **Who must execute for success?** Identify implementers whose active participation is non-negotiable. They need different engagement than oversight stakeholders.

3. **Who shapes others' opinions?** Identify influencers whose perspectives cascade through the organization. Converting one influencer can shift multiple stakeholders.

This mapping reveals where to focus effort. Priorities: convert blockers and veto holders from skeptic to supporter, move supporters to champions who actively advocate, and address concerns of implementers whose execution determines success.

Most organizations skip this step or treat it as a formality. They identify "key stakeholders" in broad terms—"finance," "operations," "sales"—without understanding specific individuals' concerns and influence. This generic approach fails because coalition building happens person by person, conversation by conversation.

> **RED FLAG: The Consensus Charade**
> **Every stakeholder "supports" the initiative** but none will commit resources or change priorities—alignment is performative, not real.
> - Stakeholders agree in meetings but don't adjust budgets or timelines
> - "Support" means attending meetings, not committing resources
> - No one pushes back publicly but nothing changes operationally
> - Initiative has universal approval and zero traction
> **Action:** Require concrete commitments (budget allocation, resource assignment, timeline changes) as the measure of alignment. Support without sacrifice isn't support—it's courtesy.

Phase 2: Individual Engagement

Schedule one-on-one conversations with each key stakeholder. These aren't presentations—they're listening sessions designed to understand perspective and address concerns.

The conversation structure is simple but disciplined: open by asking their perspective on the current problem, spend most of the time discovering their concerns and constraints, share relevant details only after you understand their viewpoint, and close by addressing their specific concerns with concrete responses.

The key is addressing real concerns with specific answers, not dismissing them as resistance to change. When the head of customer service asks "Will this replace my team?" the answer isn't "No, we're just augmenting capabilities." That's corporate speak that deepens fear. The answer must be specific: "Customer service volume grew 40% last year and your team is underwater. This handles the volume growth without proportional headcount increases. Your team shifts from routine questions to complex issues that require human judgment."

Most leaders rush these conversations or treat them as checkbox exercises. They present the AI strategy, field a few questions, and move on. Then they wonder why stakeholders aren't engaged. Real engagement takes time—usually two to four weeks of intensive one-on-one meetings before moving to formalization.

Phase 3: Coalition Formalization

Once individual alignment is sufficient, formalize the coalition through explicit mechanisms: steering committee, executive sponsor, and champion network.

The **steering committee** provides oversight, resolves issues, and makes go/no-go decisions. Keep it cross-functional with documented decision rights and explicit commitments from each member. The committee's authority must be clear—what they can decide independently versus what requires escalation.

The **executive sponsor** outranks most stakeholders to resolve disputes, cares personally about the problem being solved, commits to active involvement beyond a ceremonial title, communicates visibly and regularly about importance, and protects the initiative from competing priorities and politics. The sponsor shouldn't be the CIO—AI transformation requires business leadership, not IT leadership.

> **RED FLAG: The Delegate and Disappear**
> **Your CEO asked for quarterly updates** on AI transformation but hasn't attended a single working session—you have attention, not commitment.
> - Executive sponsor approved the budget but hasn't attended a working session
> - "Keep me updated" is the extent of leadership engagement
> - Decisions stall because the sponsor is unavailable to resolve conflicts
> - The initiative operates below the executive's attention threshold
> **Action:** Demand active sponsorship, not passive approval. Executive sponsors must attend key decision meetings, resolve cross-functional conflicts, and visibly champion the initiative. Attention without commitment is abandoned authority.

The **champion network** operates at multiple levels: executive champions who advocate in executive forums, operational champions who drive implementation, and user champions who adopt early and influence peers. Provide champions with early access to information and systems, forum for feedback and input, recognition for their support, and tools for advocacy.

Most organizations create governance structures without real authority or engagement. They hold meetings where no decisions get made, escalate issues that no one resolves, and communicate progress that no one acts on. This is governance theater—the appearance of structure without the substance of alignment.

> **RED FLAG: The Steering Committee Theater**
> **Your governance meetings** consist of status updates rather than decisions—you've built bureaucracy, not accountability.
> - Governance meetings follow the same format every time regardless of issues
> - Attendees review slides but rarely make binding decisions
> - Issues get "tabled for further discussion" meeting after meeting
> - The committee has never killed a project or redirected resources
> **Action:** Transform governance from reporting forums into decision-making bodies. Every meeting should produce explicit decisions with owners and deadlines. If governance doesn't decide, it doesn't govern.

Real coalitions have decision authority, resolve conflicts, drive execution, hold members accountable, and maintain visibility.

Phase 4: Sustaining Alignment

Coalition building isn't a one-time activity—it's a continuous discipline. Alignment erodes without active maintenance: regular stakeholder check-ins, transparent progress updates, rapid concern resolution, periodic alignment assessments, and adaptation to organizational changes.

Most organizations build coalition at launch and then neglect it. They focus on execution while alignment quietly deteriorates.

By the time they notice—usually when a key stakeholder withdraws support or funding gets cut—the damage is done.

Organizations that succeed treat coalition maintenance as operational discipline, not project overhead. They schedule it, measure it, resource it, and prioritize it even when technical work feels more urgent.

Common Alignment Failures

Three patterns kill leadership alignment with depressing regularity.

Failure Pattern 1: Executive Sponsorship Without Coalition

A senior executive declares AI transformation a strategic priority. IT launches initiatives with the sponsor's blessing. The sponsor attends the kickoff and sends supportive emails. Everything looks aligned.

Then reality hits. The CFO questions every dollar. The head of operations resists process changes. Department heads deprioritize AI for other initiatives. Frontline managers sabotage adoption through malicious compliance.

The executive sponsor grows frustrated. "I'm backing this initiative. Why isn't everyone on board?" Because sponsorship isn't coalition. Sponsorship is one person's support. Coalition is organizational commitment. The difference determines success.

Research on large-scale transformations consistently shows that executive sponsorship without cross-functional coalition fails the majority of the time. One champion can't overcome organizational resistance. You need distributed leadership—across functions, levels, and geographies.

Failure Pattern 2: Coalition Forgotten During Execution

Launch goes well. Stakeholders are engaged, the steering committee is active, champions are advocating. Then the team shifts to execution. Technical problems dominate attention. Stakeholder meetings become status updates. One-on-one conversations stop. The coalition atrophies.

Six months later, funding gets cut. The steering committee stops meeting. Champions go quiet. The initiative stalls, not because of technical failure but because the coalition collapsed while everyone was focused on delivery.

This pattern is subtle because the decay isn't dramatic. Stakeholders don't actively withdraw support—they drift. Meeting attendance drops. Response times lengthen. Competing priorities take precedence. By the time the decline is visible, reconstruction is difficult.

The solution is discipline: monthly stakeholder check-ins, quarterly alignment assessments, and rapid response to engagement drops. Coalition maintenance must be scheduled and resourced like any other operational discipline.

Failure Pattern 3: Political Naïveté

Technology leaders often dismiss organizational politics as a distraction from "real work." They focus on technical excellence and assume results speak for themselves. When political challenges surface, they're surprised and unprepared.

AI transformation is inherently political. It shifts power dynamics, threatens established authority, competes for resources, and forces trade-offs between stakeholder preferences. Pretending otherwise doesn't make it go away—it just ensures you lose the political battles.

> **RED FLAG: The Misaligned Incentives**
> **Business unit leaders** are compensated for efficiency while your AI initiative requires investment and disruption—you're asking people to work against their bonuses.
> - Leaders' performance reviews don't include AI transformation metrics
> - Short-term efficiency targets conflict with long-term capability building
> - Middle managers see AI as threat to their headcount and authority
> - No one's career advancement depends on AI initiative success
> **Action:** Align incentives explicitly. Include AI transformation objectives in leadership performance reviews. Create career paths that reward capability building. When you ask people to choose between their bonus and your initiative, the bonus wins every time.

Transformation efforts collapse when leaders fail to manage vendor influence, territorial disputes, or competing priorities. These are not technical failures—they are political failures by leaders who thought politics was beneath them.

> **RED FLAG: The Silent Saboteur**
> **Key stakeholders express support publicly** but their teams consistently miss deadlines and avoid commitment—you have malicious compliance.
> - A business unit leader "fully supports" the initiative but their team has missed every deadline

- Resources were "committed" but never actually made available
- Concerns are raised privately to peers but never surfaced in governance meetings
- Someone always has a "legitimate reason" why their deliverables are late

Action: Track actions, not words. Create visibility dashboards that show resource commitment versus actual allocation. When someone's expressed support consistently diverges from their team's behavior, address it directly. Malicious compliance is more dangerous than open opposition because it's harder to detect and impossible to work around.

Three years later, the same organization deployed a similar AI system successfully—after spending six months building coalition before writing any code. The technology was no better. The business case was no stronger. The difference was leadership alignment.

Managing Political Challenges

Even with strong coalition-building discipline, AI transformation surfaces political challenges that test leadership. Three appear with striking regularity.

Political Challenge 1: Power and Territory

AI shifts organizational power dynamics: who holds decision authority, what expertise is valued, who controls critical processes, and how success is measured.

Manifestations: Resistance from leaders whose authority is threatened. Concerns about "losing control" over processes. Fear that AI will expose performance gaps. Territorial behavior about data access.

Leadership Response: You can't eliminate these concerns—they're legitimate. You can manage them through early engagement (involve threatened stakeholders in strategy development—they're less likely to block what they helped create), shared success (structure initiatives so threatened stakeholders benefit—don't make AI a zero-sum game), executive sponsorship (ensure CEO and COO actively support transformation—political opposition collapses when executive leadership is clearly aligned), pilot projects (start with applications that help rather than threaten powerful stakeholders—build credibility before tackling sensitive areas), and transparent communication (be explicit about how AI will change roles and power dynamics—uncertainty creates resistance, clarity enables adaptation).

The common mistake is treating these concerns as irrational resistance. They're rational responses to real threats. Address them seriously or face sabotage.

Political Challenge 2: Competing Priorities

AI competes with other strategic initiatives for resources, attention, and executive focus. Budget battles erupt between AI and other technology investments. Talent gets pulled toward other strategic projects. Executive attention fragments across too many priorities. AI becomes "one of many" rather than a strategic imperative.

Leadership Response: Force clear prioritization through explicit rank-ordering of strategic initiatives. If AI isn't top three, don't pursue it seriously—you won't get the sustained executive attention required for success. Show how AI enables other strategic priorities rather than competing with them—integration, not competition. Generate visible AI value early to build momentum and justify continued investment. Secure multi-year resource commitments to avoid re-litigating AI investment annually.

The hard truth: most organizations launch too many strategic initiatives simultaneously, creating the appearance of progress while ensuring nothing succeeds. Real prioritization means saying no to good ideas so great ones get the resources they need. If your executive team can't prioritize, you can't transform.

Political Challenge 3: Vendor Influence

Vendors have sales targets, channel partnerships, and strategic objectives that may conflict with your best interests. Their proposals start driving your strategy rather than supporting it. Sales pressure creates artificial urgency. Reference customers have different situations and needs. Proprietary approaches create lock-in. Pricing models favor the vendor over the customer.

Leadership Response: Develop your AI strategy independently before engaging vendors—evaluate vendors against your strategy, not the other way around. Treat vendors as service providers, not strategic advisors—you direct, they execute. Maintain relationships with multiple vendors for critical capabilities—competition keeps vendors honest. Always have documented plan for switching vendors—knowing you can leave gives you leverage.

The vendor dynamic is subtle but powerful. Sales representatives become trusted advisors. Their proposals shape your thinking. Their roadmaps influence your strategy. Their pricing models dictate your architecture. Before you realize it, you're optimizing for vendor success rather than organizational value.

Be intentional about this dynamic. Your strategy comes first. Vendors serve it; they don't define it. Chapter 6 provides a framework for strategic vendor partnerships—the goal isn't to eliminate vendors but to ensure they strengthen your organization rather than deepen its dependence.

The Truth About Leadership Alignment

Building coalition demands time, humility, transparency, persistence, and compromise. You cannot rush stakeholder engagement. You must genuinely listen and adapt to concerns. You must share both good and bad news honestly. Alignment erodes and must be actively maintained. You cannot optimize for everyone's preferences.

But here's what matters: **Technical excellence without leadership alignment equals zero impact.** Master this pillar or accept that your AI investments will deliver minimal return.

THE BOTTOM LINE

What Matters:
Technical excellence without leadership alignment equals
zero impact. Coalition health depends on six dimensions:
stakeholder identification, coalition strength, concern
resolution, communication effectiveness, decision process,
and user voice. Most organizations score in the middle range
—sufficient to start pilots but insufficient to scale successfully.

Track This:
Coalition strength across all six dimensions using the Coalition
Strength Assessment at www.whyaifails.com. Monitor
stakeholder engagement depth, not just meeting attendance.
Track whether concerns raised in alignment sessions get
resolved. Measure decision velocity—how quickly your
coalition can make and commit to AI investment decisions.

Do This:
Map your stakeholder landscape within two weeks. Identify
the five people whose opposition would kill your AI program
and engage them individually before your next steering
committee. If your coalition is weak, invest in strengthening
alignment before encountering the political challenges that
inevitably emerge during scale. Proceeding without coalition
is expensive failure in slow motion.

Every AI initiative either builds shared commitment or
accumulates political debt. Choose deliberately.

The strongest coalition in the world can't execute what it
can't build. The next pillar, Capability Building, determines
whether your transformation creates permanent organizational
assets or temporary vendor dependencies.

Chapter Six

Capability Building—The Permanent Asset

A Fortune 500 retailer launched an AI-powered personalization initiative in 2019. The vendor delivered impressive results within six months—click-through rates rose 23%, conversion improved 18%, and revenue per visitor climbed measurably. The board was delighted. The vendor was retained.

Year two brought a 12% price increase. Reasonable enough—expanded capabilities, enhanced models. Year three: 15%. Year four: 20%. The vendor knew the retailer had no alternatives. The personalization system had become embedded in the customer experience. Replacing it would mean temporary performance degradation that would alarm investors. The vendor had the leverage, and they used it.

By year five, the retailer was paying 2.8 times the original contract value for what had become table-stakes capability. Competitors had similar systems. The competitive advantage had evaporated, but costs kept climbing. Worse: the retailer's internal team had learned almost nothing transferable. They could configure the vendor's platform, submit support tickets, and monitor dashboards. They couldn't build similar capabilities, evaluate alternatives, or negotiate from strength.

They didn't build an AI system. They rented one indefinitely.

This is what happens when organizations optimize for deployment speed over capability building. Every AI investment your organization makes either builds a permanent asset or accumulates an expensive dependency. The difference isn't in the technology you choose or the vendors you hire—it's in whether your organization emerges from each initiative more capable than before.

The Capability Imperative: Why Vendors Can't Save You

The majority who fail don't recognize this pattern until it's too late. They optimize for speed-to-value, choose vendors who handle everything, and measure success by deployment velocity. They celebrate fast pilot launches while building no internal understanding of how anything works. Years later, they're trapped—dependent on vendors who set prices, control roadmaps, and constrain strategic flexibility.

The disciplined minority take a different approach. They treat every AI initiative as an opportunity to build organizational capability, not just deploy technology. They structure vendor relationships to transfer knowledge, not replace it. They measure success not just by what systems do, but by what their organization learns. They distinguish between renting functionality and building assets.

The difference becomes stark over time. Organizations with high capability readiness—the ability to understand, modify, and potentially rebuild systems without vendor assistance— consistently show dramatically lower total cost of ownership and faster innovation cycles than those with low readiness. The gap widens each year as capable organizations compound learning while dependent organizations accumulate costs.

Capability building isn't about rejecting vendors or insisting on building everything in-house. It's about ensuring every AI investment makes your organization more capable—whether you build, buy, or partner. Every initiative should answer one question: "If this vendor disappeared tomorrow, what organizational capability would we retain?"

Most organizations can't answer it. They can describe what their systems do but not how they work. They can report on ROI but not on knowledge gained. They can list deployed solutions but not explain what makes them more capable than before they started.

True organizational capability means you can evaluate AI opportunities and vendor claims independently, implement solutions with appropriate vendor support but not dependency, operate and improve systems over time, adapt to changing technology and business needs, make informed build-versus-buy decisions, and capture learning that compounds with each initiative.

This chapter provides the framework for building that capability systematically. It won't happen by accident. It requires intentional strategy across five dimensions: talent development, vendor partnerships, knowledge management, infrastructure decisions, and organizational learning culture.

Master these dimensions, and AI becomes a permanent asset that increases in value over time. Skip them, and you're building an expensive dependency that constrains your future.

The Capability Building Framework

Building lasting capability requires intentional strategy across five dimensions. These aren't sequential phases but parallel efforts that reinforce each other.

Dimension 1: Strategic Talent Development

The foundation of capability is people who can think independently about AI opportunities and challenges. This doesn't mean hiring a team of PhD data scientists—it means developing the right expertise mix for your organization's maturity and ambition.

Most organizations make one of two hiring errors: they over-hire expensive talent for capabilities they don't yet need, or under-hire junior staff who lack the experience to succeed. Both waste resources and slow capability development.

The strategic approach matches talent strategy to organizational maturity.

Early Stage (Months 0–12): Start with one or two experienced "translators" who bridge business and technical domains. These people can evaluate vendors critically, design pilot approaches, build initial frameworks, and mentor less experienced team members. They don't need to be cutting-edge researchers—they need breadth, business acumen, and the ability to build capability in others. Look for professionals who have implemented AI in production, understand the gap between pilot and scale, and can explain technical concepts to business leaders without jargon.

Growth Stage (Months 12–24): Add domain-specific specialists as patterns emerge. Data engineers who build infrastructure supporting multiple use cases. ML engineers who move pilots to production and maintain deployed systems. Domain experts who understand both AI techniques and your business context deeply enough to identify high-value opportunities. Hire for proven patterns you're ready to scale, not speculative capabilities you might need someday.

Scale Stage (Months 24+): Expand capacity in areas demonstrating sustained value. Build bench strength with mixed experience levels—senior practitioners who can handle complex challenges, mid-level engineers who can execute independently, and junior staff who can grow into specialized roles. Create career paths that retain talent by offering both technical tracks to principal/fellow roles and management tracks to director levels.

But hiring is only part of talent strategy. Development matters more. Identify high-potential employees interested in AI and give them paths to contribute. Create training programs that develop specific skills your organization needs. Establish rotations where engineers from different backgrounds cross-pollinate knowledge. Pair junior staff with experienced mentors who accelerate learning. Reward knowledge sharing and documentation as much as individual achievement.

Organizations that invest in systematic internal development —not hiring alone—show faster capability growth and better retention than those focused solely on external recruitment. Industry research consistently confirms that organizations with mature AI practices prioritize internal skill development alongside hiring. Internal development builds loyalty, creates institutional knowledge, and grows people who understand your business context deeply.

The goal isn't to build the largest AI team—it's to develop enough internal expertise to evaluate options independently, implement strategically, operate sustainably, and learn continuously.

> **RED FLAG: The Hiring Lottery**
>
> Your talent strategy is a lottery if:
>
> - You're posting for "unicorn" candidates who are simultaneously ML engineers, business strategists, and domain experts
> - You're offering above-market salaries but no clear career path or development roadmap
> - AI talent turnover exceeds 40% within eighteen months of hiring
> - Your job descriptions read like wishlists rather than realistic role definitions
> - You're solving capability gaps purely through hiring without building systematic internal development pathways
>
> **Action:** Audit your last five AI hires. If more than half left within eighteen months or were hired for roles that didn't match organizational maturity, redesign your talent strategy around systematic development pathways rather than hoping the next hire will be a unicorn.

Dimension 2: Strategic Vendor Partnerships

Vendors are necessary but must be engaged strategically—to build capability, not dependency. The key is structuring relationships where knowledge transfer is explicit, not incidental.

Define capability goals before selecting vendors. What skills do you want to develop internally? What are you comfortable outsourcing long-term? How will you ensure knowledge transfer happens? What prevents lock-in? These questions should shape vendor selection criteria and contract terms, not surface as afterthoughts once deals are signed.

Make capability building explicit in contracts. Require vendors to train internal staff as a deliverable. Include specific knowledge transfer requirements—documentation to your standards, code review sessions, architecture reviews, operational runbooks. Specify what intellectual property and artifacts the organization retains. Define criteria for reducing vendor involvement over time. Make these contractual obligations, not hopeful expectations.

Structure engagements as co-development, not observation. Your team members should be embedded in delivery doing real work, not providing oversight or attending status meetings. Conduct joint technical reviews where vendors explain decisions and alternatives considered. Use pair programming or collaborative development sessions. Give your team ownership of components they'll maintain post-deployment. Accept that this approach slows initial delivery—you're optimizing for capability building, not deployment speed.

Maintain multi-vendor strategies to avoid single-vendor dependency. Use different vendors for different use cases so no single relationship becomes critical. Ensure solutions work across multiple platforms rather than locking into proprietary ecosystems. Build internal expertise in integration and orchestration that persists regardless of which vendors you use.

Negotiate contracts that limit lock-in through clear data ownership, export capabilities, and termination provisions.

Plan exit strategies from the start. Every vendor relationship should include clear answers: What would it take to transition away? What internal capabilities would we need? What alternatives exist? How do we maintain flexibility to switch if strategic priorities or commercial terms change?

The vendor engagement spectrum runs from full independence to complete dependency:

Capability Builder Engagement: Vendor acts as teacher and partner. Joint development with explicit knowledge transfer. Time-boxed engagement designed to build internal capability. Success measured by reduced vendor dependency over time. Appropriate for capabilities you'll need repeatedly and want to own strategically.

Knowledge Transfer Engagement: Vendor implements but internal team learns alongside. Documentation and training mandatory deliverables. Your team takes ownership at completion. Follow-on support available but not required. Appropriate when building in-house takes too long but you want ultimate independence.

Service Provider Engagement: Vendor owns implementation and operation long-term. Your team provides business requirements and oversight. Knowledge transfer not primary goal. Appropriate for commodity capabilities not core to competitive advantage—but acknowledge you're creating a dependency, not building an asset.

Most organizations default to service provider engagements for everything, optimizing for short-term delivery speed at the cost of long-term capability. The strategic approach matches engagement type to strategic importance and builds toward independence where it matters.

Dimension 3: Knowledge Management Systems

Individual expertise is fragile. When people leave—and they will—organizational capability shouldn't walk out the door with them. Knowledge management converts individual learning into institutional assets.

Set documentation standards before starting projects, not after. Define what good documentation looks like. Create templates for architecture decisions, implementation approaches, lessons learned, and operational procedures. Make documentation a required deliverable for every initiative, reviewed with the same rigor as code or business results.

Build pattern libraries that capture reusable solutions to common problems. When you solve a problem once—how to deploy a model, handle data quality issues, integrate with specific systems—document the pattern so the next team doesn't start from zero. Organize patterns by domain, technical area, and business context. Make finding and applying existing patterns faster than reinventing them.

Create learning loops that convert experience to knowledge systematically. After every pilot, conduct structured retrospectives that capture what worked, what didn't, and what would be done differently. Document technical decisions and trade-offs, not just outcomes. Share lessons across teams through regular forums, not just documentation repositories. Make learning from others' experience culturally normal.

Establish communities of practice where practitioners share knowledge, solve problems collaboratively, and develop standards. These forums shouldn't be top-down mandates—they should grow from genuine desire to learn from each other. Support them with time, tools, and recognition, but let practitioners drive content and direction.

Organizations with systematic knowledge capture achieve faster time-to-value on subsequent projects than those without structured knowledge systems. The investment in knowledge management pays compounding dividends.

The goal is institutional memory that survives turnover—documented patterns, shared understanding, and cultural norms that new team members can absorb quickly.

RED FLAG: The Training Theater
Your training program is theater if:
- AI training consists primarily of vendor-led product training disguised as capability building
- You track course completion rates but never measure whether participants apply what they learned
- Teams attend workshops and earn certifications but cannot apply concepts to actual projects
- Training budgets are spent on generic "Introduction to AI" courses year after year
- Leadership points to training hours as evidence of capability building while project outcomes haven't improved

Action: Survey your AI practitioners: ask them to name one specific skill they gained from formal training that they applied to a real project in the past six months. If most cannot answer, redesign your training around applied, project-based learning tied to actual business challenges rather than generic coursework.

Dimension 4: Strategic Infrastructure Decisions

Infrastructure choices create or constrain long-term flexibility. The wrong foundation leads to vendor lock-in regardless of how good your team becomes.

Prioritize interoperability over optimization. Choose platforms that integrate well with others rather than those claiming best-in-class performance through proprietary approaches. Accept modest performance trade-offs for strategic flexibility. The ability to switch platforms or integrate new capabilities matters more than marginal efficiency gains in isolated components.

Maintain platform independence where possible. Use abstraction layers that insulate applications from underlying platform specifics. Avoid deep dependencies on vendor-specific APIs unless switching costs are acceptable. Design for portability even if you don't plan to switch—the ability to leave provides negotiating leverage and protects against adverse vendor behavior.

Own your data completely. Ensure you can export it in usable formats at any time. Maintain copies in systems you control, not just vendor platforms. Define data governance policies that preserve your rights regardless of vendor relationships. Design systems so data remains accessible even if vendors disappear.

Make build-versus-buy decisions strategically, not arbitrarily. Build capabilities that are core to competitive advantage— differentiating and strategic—regardless of whether building costs more initially. Buy or partner on commodity capabilities where differentiation doesn't matter and vendor solutions are genuinely good enough. But even when buying, structure relationships to preserve flexibility and prevent lock-in.

The principle: make infrastructure decisions that maximize future options rather than optimize for current constraints. You don't know what you'll need in three years—preserve flexibility to adapt.

Dimension 5: Organizational Learning Culture

Capability building fails without a culture that values learning over perfection, sharing over hoarding, and adaptation over rigidity.

Normalize learning from failure. When pilots fail—and some will—conduct thorough retrospectives focused on learning, not blame. Make failure analysis public and celebrate it when lessons are captured well. Organizations that punish failure get hidden failures and no learning. Organizations that reward learning from failure get transparency and compounding improvement.

Create forums for cross-functional learning where business and technical teams share perspectives. Technical teams learn business context and constraints. Business teams grasp technical possibilities and limitations. This cross-pollination surfaces high-value opportunities and prevents ivory-tower syndrome—AI teams building impressive technology nobody uses.

Recognize and reward knowledge contribution as much as individual achievement. Celebrate people who document patterns, mentor others, or solve problems benefiting multiple teams—not just those who ship features. If your promotion system only values individual output, knowledge hoarding becomes rational and capability building fails.

Encourage strategic external engagement—conference talks, publications, open-source contributions—that builds your organization's reputation and attracts talent. People who teach externally learn deeply and bring outside perspectives back. Organizations that encourage this benefit from network effects and stronger recruiting.

Research on AI adoption consistently finds that organizations with strong learning cultures achieve significantly higher pilot-to-production success rates. Culture either enables capability building or ensures its failure—regardless of how much you invest in people, vendors, knowledge systems, or infrastructure.

The goal is making organizational learning inevitable through culture, not dependent on individual initiative or heroic effort.

RED FLAG: The Perpetual Beginner
Your organization is stuck in perpetual beginner mode if:

- Every new AI initiative starts from scratch with no reference to previous project learnings

- There is no institutional memory from prior pilots—no documented patterns, no reusable architectures, no lessons-learned library

- The same "getting started with AI" conversations repeat annually with new stakeholders or new vendors

- Teams cannot point to specific capabilities that compounded from one initiative to the next

- Leadership treats each AI project as a standalone experiment rather than a step in a capability-building journey

Action: Map your last three AI initiatives chronologically. Identify what specific capability each one built that the next

> one leveraged. If the answer is "nothing"—each started from zero—establish a mandatory lessons-learned capture process and a pattern library that makes reuse the default, not the exception.

Capability in Action: Tale of Two Organizations

Two mid-sized manufacturers with similar business models launched AI initiatives within months of each other. Both chose the same vendor. Five years later, their situations couldn't be more different.

Organization A: The Vendor-Dependent Path

Started strong. Signed a comprehensive services agreement for demand forecasting. The vendor promised a turnkey solution —data integration, model development, deployment, and ongoing operation. Timeline: seven months to production.

The organization provided business requirements and data access. The vendor did everything else. Launch went smoothly. Forecasting accuracy improved measurably. The business was delighted. Contract extended to inventory optimization. Then supply chain. Then production scheduling.

By year three, the vendor was running critical business processes. The internal team consisted of business analysts who defined requirements and project managers who coordinated with the vendor. Nobody understood how the systems worked. Nobody could modify logic without vendor involvement. Nobody could evaluate whether the vendor's approach was optimal or merely adequate.

Year four brought a 20% price increase. The vendor knew they were embedded in critical operations. Replacing them would take eighteen months minimum and disrupt operations unacceptably. The organization negotiated but had no leverage. They paid.

Year five: another increase, plus the vendor started pushing their new platform requiring migration and additional fees. The organization is now paying 3.4 times their original contract value. They can't switch—too embedded, too risky. They can't negotiate—no alternatives. They built no capability. They have an expensive dependency that will only get worse.

Organization B: The Co-Development Path

Took a different approach from day one. Negotiated a co-development engagement where the vendor would build the initial system but transfer knowledge systematically. Timeline ran longer—eleven months rather than seven—and cost more upfront. But the goal was capability building, not deployment speed.

Their internal team embedded in development alongside the vendor. The vendor explained architecture decisions, conducted code reviews, documented patterns, and trained staff on maintenance and extension. At deployment, Organization B's team could operate the system independently and modify it without vendor involvement.

For the second project—inventory optimization—vendor involvement dropped to 60%. Internal team owned more of the implementation, with vendor providing guidance and specialized expertise. Third project: vendor involvement dropped to 40%. Internal team led implementation with vendor as advisor.

By year four, Organization B was implementing most projects internally with occasional vendor consultation on specialized capabilities. Year five: they were teaching other organizations their approach and had become industry thought leaders in practical AI implementation.

Total cost over five years: 40% less than Organization A despite the higher initial investment. More importantly, they built permanent organizational capability. They evaluate new vendors objectively. They implement solutions themselves. They negotiate from strength when vendor partnerships make sense. They own their AI strategy rather than being owned by vendor relationships.

The difference wasn't technology—both organizations used similar platforms. The difference was strategic intent from the beginning. One optimized for deployment speed. The other optimized for capability building. One built an asset. The other accumulated a liability.

Common Capability Building Mistakes

Most organizations fail at capability building in predictable patterns. Recognizing these mistakes is the first step to avoiding them.

Mistake 1: The Vendor Dependency Trap

Pattern: Start with a vendor to accelerate initial projects. Vendor delivers successfully. Extend the relationship. Never build internal capability. Years later, discover the vendor owns your AI strategy.

Why It Happens: Speed-to-value pressure. Signing vendor contracts is easier than building internal capability. Early project success masks the long-term dependency forming underneath. By the time costs escalate, switching is too painful.

Prevention: Structure initial vendor engagements explicitly for knowledge transfer. Accept slower initial delivery. Measure capability building alongside business value. Ask "vendor disappears" question regularly.

Action: Restructure vendor engagements to require knowledge transfer milestones. Accept slower initial delivery in exchange for building internal capability. If your team can't operate the system independently within twelve months, the engagement is building dependency, not capability.

> **RED FLAG: The Vendor Dependency Death Spiral**
> Your vendor relationship has evolved from partnership to captivity:
> - Initial vendor engagement was never structured for knowledge transfer
> - Internal teams cannot operate, modify, or extend vendor-built systems independently
> - Vendor costs escalate annually with no competitive leverage
> - When asked "What happens if this vendor disappears?" leadership has no answer
>
> **Action:** Make documentation a mandatory deliverable for every AI initiative. Require pair programming and cross-training as standard practice. If your AI capability walks out the door when one person leaves, you don't have organizational capability—you have individual dependency.

Mistake 2: The Expertise Exodus

Pattern: Hire talented people. They build critical systems. Knowledge stays in their heads. They leave. Capability leaves with them. The remaining team can operate systems but can't understand, modify, or extend them.

Why It Happens: Documentation deferred. Knowledge sharing not systematically valued. Individuals rewarded for heroic effort, not for teaching others. Leadership assumes people will stay forever.

Warning Signs:

- Critical systems only one or two people understand

- Panic when key people give notice

- New team members take three or more months to contribute meaningfully

- No written architecture documentation or decision records

- Knowledge transfer happens through osmosis, not process

Prevention: Make documentation a mandatory deliverable. Make pair programming and cross-training standard practice. Rotate people across projects. Value knowledge sharing explicitly in performance reviews.

Mistake 3: The Theory-Practice Gap

Pattern: Hire for academic credentials—PhDs, research publications, cutting-edge expertise. Team builds impressive prototypes. Nothing reaches production. A gap opens between research capability and production deployment expertise.

Why It Happens: Over-indexing on academic achievement. Undervaluing production engineering experience. Assuming smart people can figure out deployment. Failing to recognize that research skills differ from production skills.

Prevention: Hire for production experience, not research pedigree. Balance PhDs with engineers who have shipped systems. Value "made it work reliably in production" over "published impressive paper." For most organizations, production capability matters more than research capability.

Mistake 4: The Ivory Tower

Pattern: Build a capable AI team. They disconnect from business priorities. They build impressive technology that solves problems nobody has. The business stops taking their work to production. The AI team becomes marginalized despite strong technical capability.

Why It Happens: AI team prizes technical sophistication over business value. No systematic connection to business priorities. Reward systems favor complexity over practical impact. Distance grows between what the team builds and what the business needs.

Warning Signs:

- Business requests help but AI team says they're "working on more important things"

- AI team demos impressive technology that solves problems nobody has

- Pilots completed but business won't take them to production

- Growing gap between what AI team builds and what business needs

- Requests for simple automation go unfilled while complex research continues

Prevention: Embed AI team members with business units. Make business impact the primary success metric. Hold regular forums where business leaders describe pain points directly. Rotate team members through business roles. Don't tolerate technical excellence that delivers no business value.

Mistake 5: The Build Everything Approach

Pattern: Reject vendors entirely. Insist on building everything in-house. Reinvent wheels unnecessarily. Fall behind competitors who use strategic partnerships. Build technical capability but fail to deliver business value fast enough.

Why It Happens: Overreaction to vendor dependency concerns. Pride in technical capability. Failure to distinguish commodity from differentiating capabilities. Not-invented-here syndrome.

Prevention: Strategic build-versus-buy framework. Build differentiating capabilities in-house. Partner on commodity capabilities. Measure capability building and business delivery. Recognize that learning to integrate strategically is itself a capability.

Capability Maturity Assessment

Diagnosing your organization's capability maturity requires honest evaluation across five dimensions: strategic talent development, strategic vendor partnerships, knowledge management systems, strategic infrastructure, and learning culture.

The complete Capability Maturity Assessment—with twenty scored questions, benchmarks, and targeted recommendations—is available at **www.whyaifails.com**. Use it to identify where capability building needs focus. Most organizations score lowest on vendor partnership strategy and knowledge management—the dimensions that separate building assets from accumulating liabilities.

THE BOTTOM LINE

What Matters:
Every AI investment should make your organization more capable—able to evaluate options independently, implement strategically, operate sustainably, and learn continuously. Capability compounds over time. Dependency constrains your future. The difference between organizations that succeed and those that fail isn't technology or talent—it's whether AI investments build capability or rent functionality.

Track This:
Capability maturity across five dimensions: talent development, vendor partnerships, knowledge management, infrastructure independence, and learning culture. Use the capability readiness test for every vendor relationship: if this vendor disappeared tomorrow, what organizational capability would you retain? Track what your organization learns, not just what systems deliver. Measure capability growth alongside business value.

Do This:
Audit current vendor relationships within thirty days—restructure contracts to require explicit knowledge transfer. Invest in knowledge management infrastructure before you need it. Hire and develop strategically for your organization's current maturity, not aspirational future state. Accept slower initial progress to build permanent capability. Master capability building and each initiative makes the next one easier. Capability is the permanent asset. Everything else is temporary.

You've established strategic clarity that guides AI investments. You've built leadership alignment that sustains transformation despite pressure. You've developed organizational capability that makes you vendor-independent and strategically flexible.

Internal capability gives you the foundation. But even capable organizations waste resources without disciplined experimentation. The next challenge is pilot discipline—the framework that separates productive pilots from zombie projects consuming resources indefinitely.

Strategy, alignment, and capability mean nothing if your pilots never generate the evidence you need to scale or stop. The next chapter addresses how to run experiments that produce clear decisions within ninety days rather than drifting for years without resolution.

Chapter Seven

Pilot Discipline—The Experimentation Framework

The director of AI looked tired. The team was eighteen months into what was supposed to be a three-month pilot.

"How's the customer service chatbot performing?" the CIO asked.

"Really well. The team loves working on it. We've learned so much about natural language processing and our knowledge base architecture. The accuracy scores are impressive—87% on our test set."

"What's the business impact?"

He paused. "We're still measuring that. The pilot population is small, so it's hard to isolate the signal. But user feedback is positive."

"When do you decide whether to scale it or kill it?"

Another pause. "We haven't defined that yet. We're still gathering learnings."

This is how organizations bleed resources. Not through spectacular failures but through pilots that never die. They consume budgets, occupy talented teams, and deliver nothing meaningful—yet continue indefinitely because no one established clear criteria for success or failure.

These are **zombie pilots**—technically alive but not functioning. They shamble through organizations, consuming resources while delivering no production value. Every organization accumulates them. Most have dozens.

Pilot discipline—the fourth pillar—means killing zombies before they spread and treating new pilots as experiments with clear hypotheses, success criteria, and decision points rather than innovation theater disguised as learning.

The Zombie Epidemic

Here's the typical decay pattern:

Month 0—The Launch: Excitement everywhere. Press releases tout innovation. Executives attend the kickoff. The team is energized and optimistic.

Month 3—Promising Results: The technical team demos the system. It works—sort of. Accuracy is decent. A few people use it. Results are "promising" and "show potential."

Month 6—Quiet Concerns: Usage is lower than hoped. Results are mixed. Technical issues have emerged. But the team is "iterating" and "learning valuable lessons" about the problem space.

Month 9—The Awkward Phase: No one wants to discuss the pilot. It's still running. Some people use it occasionally. When pressed, the team says they're "optimizing" and "enhancing capabilities."

Month 12—Zombie Status: The pilot has become background noise. It's in the portfolio but driving no value. No one can kill it ("we're learning!") but no one wants to scale it ("results are mixed!").

Month 18+—The Walking Dead: The pilot continues indefinitely. Original champions have moved on. New leaders inherit it but don't understand the context. It persists because stopping requires someone to admit failure.

The waste is staggering. Industry research consistently shows that fewer than one in four AI pilots reaches production scale. Most run nine to twelve months or longer, and organizations typically carry three to five times more pilots than they can effectively support. Fewer than a third of organizations establish explicit go/no-go criteria before launching AI pilots.

But the real cost isn't financial—it's opportunity cost. Resources trapped in zombie pilots could fund production systems that deliver value. Every dollar and hour invested in a pilot that will never scale is stolen from initiatives that could succeed.

Innovation Theater vs. Scientific Experimentation

The root cause of zombies: treating pilots as demonstrations of innovation rather than scientific experiments designed to test specific hypotheses about business value.

Innovation Theater looks like this:

- **Goal:** Show we're doing AI
- **Success:** Technically working system
- **Timeline:** Open-ended "until we learn enough"
- **Metrics:** Accuracy scores and technical performance
- **Decision:** Implicit—"we'll know when it's ready"

Scientific Experimentation looks like this:

- **Goal:** Test specific hypothesis about business value
- **Success:** Meeting predefined business outcome criteria
- **Timeline:** Fixed duration with hard deadline
- **Metrics:** Business impact with clear thresholds
- **Decision:** Explicit go/no-go based on defined criteria

The difference is fundamental. Innovation theater can never fail because any result counts as "learning." Scientific experiments must be falsifiable—there must be results that would prove the hypothesis wrong.

Example of real hypothesis formation:

"We hypothesize that ML-based lead scoring will improve sales conversion rates from 3.2% to 4.5% within three months because it will identify buying signals our manual process misses, allowing sales reps to focus time on highest-probability opportunities."

Not: *"Let's explore how AI could help sales."*

The first statement makes specific, testable predictions. If conversion rates don't reach at least 4.0% (minimum success threshold), the hypothesis is false. Period. The team makes a go/no-go decision based on data, not sentiment.

The second statement justifies unlimited investment and timeline. Any result—even outright failure—can be framed as valuable learning.

In martial arts, sparring sessions have a clear purpose—test a specific technique, develop a specific response. A sparring session without objectives is just fighting. Pilots without hypotheses and kill criteria are just spending.

Scientific experimentation requires four elements:

1. **Clear Hypothesis:** Every pilot tests a specific claim about business value. Not "AI can help with X" but "AI will improve metric Y from A to B by doing Z."

2. **Testable Predictions:** The hypothesis makes predictions you can verify within a defined timeframe. Specific metrics will improve by specific amounts under specific conditions.

3. **Falsifiability:** There must be results that would prove the hypothesis wrong. If those thresholds aren't met, the pilot fails. This clarity prevents zombie pilots.

4. **Defined Decision Points:** Before starting, establish when decisions will be made, who has authority to decide, what criteria drive decisions, and what happens after each possible outcome.

Most pilots lack this clarity. They're designed to avoid failure rather than generate clear go/no-go signals.

The Go/No-Go Framework

Effective pilots follow a disciplined framework—not a bureaucratic process, but a structure that accelerates learning and prevents resource waste.

Phase 1: Pilot Design (Two to Four Weeks)

Before writing code, invest in rigorous planning:

Business Case: What problem costs the organization money or opportunity today? What's the quantified cost? What improvement would AI deliver? What's the financial value of that improvement?

Hypothesis Statement: Write it explicitly: "We hypothesize that [AI approach] will improve [specific metric] from [current baseline] to [target level] within [timeframe] because [mechanism of improvement]."

Three-Level Success Criteria:

- **Minimum Success:** The go/no-go threshold. What must be achieved to justify scaling? Usually: ROI positive within twelve to eighteen months.

- **Target Success:** The planned outcome from your business case.

- **Exceptional Success:** Results that significantly exceed expectations.

Define these before starting. Reaches minimum success? Scale. Below minimum? Kill. This removes politics from the decision.

Metrics Framework: For each success level, define leading indicators (early signals like adoption rates) and lagging indicators (ultimate business outcomes like revenue impact). Document how each metric will be measured, the current baseline, and measurement frequency.

Deliberate Constraints: Keep pilots small enough to fail cheaply but large enough to generate meaningful signal. Typically ten to fifty users, two to four months, minimal integration, constrained use case.

Decision Framework: Document who makes the go/no-go decision, what happens if stakeholders disagree, how quickly the decision will be made after pilot completion, and how results will be communicated regardless of outcome.

> **RED FLAG: The Perfect Conditions Fallacy**
> **Your pilot worked beautifully** with curated data and dedicated support but fails with real users and messy inputs—you tested a demo, not a solution.
> Your pilot is hiding behind perfect conditions if:
> - Pilot uses cleaned, curated data that doesn't represent production reality
> - Dedicated team provides support that won't exist at scale
> - Users were hand-selected enthusiasts, not skeptical end-users
> - Environment was controlled in ways production never will be
> **Action:** Design pilots to encounter real-world friction. Use production-representative data, include skeptical users, and limit support to what's sustainable at scale. A pilot that only works under perfect conditions isn't proving viability—it's proving fragility.

Phase 2: Pilot Execution (Two to Four Months)

Execute with discipline:

Fixed Timeline: Time-boxing forces focus. Resist extensions except for documented reasons beyond the team's control. Pilots that run indefinitely become zombies.

Weekly Measurement: Track both leading and lagging indicators. Leading indicators should show progress within two to four weeks. Document positive and negative results honestly. Hiding problems doesn't make them disappear.

Bi-Weekly Reviews: Steering committee checks progress, removes blockers, but doesn't change scope or success criteria. These reviews keep pilots visible and accountable.

Issue Escalation: When blockers emerge that threaten timeline or success, escalate immediately. Don't let pilots drift silently into trouble.

Learning Capture: Document what's working and what isn't in real-time. Don't wait until the end to capture insights. The best learning often comes from unexpected problems.

Phase 3: Decision Point (One to Two Weeks)

After pilot completion, make rapid decisions:

Results Package: Present actual results against each success criterion. Show quantitative metrics and qualitative insights. Include positive and negative findings. Be honest about what worked and what didn't.

Three Decision Options:

1. **Scale:** Minimum success achieved or exceeded. Move to production deployment.

2. **Iterate:** Shows promise but didn't reach minimum. Run another time-boxed pilot with a different approach. Requires new hypothesis and success criteria.

3. **Kill:** Didn't reach minimum success and no clear path to improvement. Terminate and reallocate resources.

No fourth option. No indefinite extensions. No retroactive lowering of success criteria. Make the hard decision.

Decision Timeline: Two weeks maximum from pilot completion to decision. Longer delays allow politics to trump data.

Communication: Announce the decision with clear rationale. If killing, acknowledge the team's effort and the learning captured. If scaling, document next steps. Either way, be transparent.

> **RED FLAG: The Immortal Pilot**
> Your pilot is already a zombie if:
> - Running >90 days without scheduled go/no-go decision
> - Success criteria have changed since launch
> - Decision meeting has been postponed 2+ times
> - Team discussing "Phase 2 pilot" without Phase 1 decision
> - Executive sponsor changed or disengaged
> - Metrics trending away from targets
> - No one can articulate what would trigger a kill decision
> **Action:** Force decision within 14 days. Scale, iterate with new timeline, or kill. No fourth option.

Phase 4: Learning Integration (One Week)

Whether scaling or killing, capture lessons:

What Worked: Document practices, decisions, or approaches that drove success. Make these repeatable.

What Didn't: Document failures, missteps, or wrong assumptions. Prevent repetition.

Unexpected Learnings: Capture surprises, positive or negative. These often yield the most valuable insights.

Process Improvements: Based on this pilot, what would you change in the pilot framework itself? Update templates and checklists accordingly.

Knowledge Sharing: Brief other teams on key learnings. Build organizational capability by spreading knowledge.

> **RED FLAG: The Success Criteria Shuffle**
> **Initial metrics weren't met** so you introduced new measures to demonstrate progress—you're lying with statistics.
> Your pilot is shuffling success criteria if:
> - Original success criteria were quietly replaced with new metrics after the first review
> - Team celebrates "directional improvement" when targets were missed by wide margins
> - Every quarterly review introduces a new way to measure the same pilot
> - No one can articulate what specific outcome the pilot was supposed to achieve
>
> **Action:** Lock success criteria at pilot launch. If the metrics don't show what you need, that's information—not an invitation to find friendlier numbers. Changing the goalposts mid-game isn't adaptation; it's deception that delays the kill decision every failing pilot needs.

Three Common Pilot Failures

Even with good intentions, pilots fail in predictable patterns:

The Zombie Pilot

Symptom: Pilot runs indefinitely without clear decision or production deployment. Team claims continued "learning" but delivers no business value.

Root Cause: No predefined success criteria or decision authority. The career risk of admitting failure exceeds the cost of maintaining the pilot.

Consequence: Resources trapped indefinitely. Opportunity cost compounds. Other initiatives starve for budget and talent.

Solution: Establish go/no-go criteria and decision timeline before launch. Empower someone to kill failing pilots. Celebrate learning from failures as much as successes.

The Moving Target

Symptom: Success criteria change during the pilot. When original metrics aren't met, new metrics are defined to show success.

Root Cause: Lack of discipline and commitment to original hypothesis. Political pressure to avoid failure. Insufficient upfront rigor.

Consequence: Pilots never fail because goalposts move. Resources stay trapped. Real learning is impossible when criteria are fluid.

Solution: Lock success criteria before pilot launch. Changes require steering committee approval and pilot clock reset. Track original metrics regardless.

The Feature Factory

Symptom: Pilot scope expands continuously. New capabilities added before the original hypothesis is tested. Timeline extends indefinitely.

Root Cause: Confusing pilots with product development. Inability to resist "wouldn't it be cool if..." thinking.

Consequence: The original question never gets answered. Complexity increases. Timeline stretches. The original hypothesis gets buried.

Solution: Freeze scope at launch. Additional features go in the backlog for future pilots. Finish testing the hypothesis you started with.

> **RED FLAG: The Feature Creep Spiral**
> **Pilot scope expanded three times** and timeline doubled—you've converted a learning experiment into a development project.
> Your pilot has entered the feature creep spiral if:
> - Original ninety-day pilot is now approaching month 8
> - Requirements document has grown from one page to fifteen
> - "Just one more feature" has been said more than three times
> - Team can't articulate what the pilot is specifically testing anymore
>
> **Action:** Lock pilot scope at launch. Any scope change triggers a formal go/no-go decision on the original scope first. Expanding scope without deciding on the original experiment means you're avoiding judgment, not improving the pilot.

What Killing Pilots Actually Looks Like

A large retail organization had twenty-three active AI pilots. Most had been running over a year. Some exceeded two years. In the first honest portfolio review, the room went quiet when someone asked the team to name one pilot that had reached production. The silence lasted long enough that someone coughed.

Leadership applied the pilot discipline framework rigorously. They defined success criteria for each pilot retroactively. They gave teams sixty days to demonstrate minimum success or recommend termination.

They killed nineteen of the twenty-three pilots.

The CFO was horrified. "We've invested millions in those initiatives. How can we just walk away?"

"The investment is gone," the CIO replied. "It's a sunk cost. The only question is whether we keep investing in initiatives that will never deliver production value. Every dollar we spend on zombies is stolen from the four pilots that show real promise."

They terminated the nineteen and fully resourced the four survivors. Within six months, two reached production. Within a year, all four were delivering measurable business value.

The four successful pilots generated more value than all twenty-three combined had produced in two years of experimentation.

That's the power of pilot discipline. Not just preventing zombies—concentrating resources on initiatives that work.

The nineteen teams whose pilots were terminated? Within three months, every team member was reallocated to initiatives with clearer paths to value. Morale improved. People prefer working on things that matter to maintaining zombies.

The Courage to Kill

Here's the uncomfortable truth: killing pilots demands courage that most organizations lack.

It means admitting that smart people invested significant time and money in something that didn't work. It means telling executives that their championed initiative failed. It means accepting sunk costs and resisting the temptation to extend "just a bit longer" to avoid confronting failure.

The majority who fail lack this courage. They create cultures where pilots never die—they just fade into zombiehood. Resources get trapped. Innovation slows. The organization accumulates a portfolio of initiatives that consume budget while delivering nothing.

Organizations that succeed understand that **killing failed pilots is as important as scaling successful ones.** Both demand discipline. Both demand courage. Both separate learning organizations from those that merely appear to be learning.

Your organization has zombie pilots right now. Probably dozens. The question isn't whether they exist—it's whether you have the courage to kill them.

> **RED FLAG: The Kill Authority Vacuum**
> **Nobody has explicit authority** to terminate pilots, so every mediocre experiment lives forever.
> Your pilot governance has a kill authority vacuum if:
> - No single person or committee has been designated as the "kill authority"
> - Termination requires consensus from multiple stakeholders who all avoid being the decider
> - Failing pilots get "extended for further evaluation" rather than terminated
> - The organization has never formally killed an AI pilot
> **Action:** Designate explicit kill authority before any pilot launches. One person or committee must have the power—and the expectation—to terminate initiatives that don't meet criteria. Organizations that can't kill pilots can't learn from them.

Pilot Discipline Assessment

How disciplined is your organization's approach to pilots? The Pilot Discipline Assessment evaluates six dimensions: hypothesis clarity, success criteria definition, timeline discipline, decision process rigor, kill rate, and learning capture. Most organizations score below 18 out of 30. The assessment is designed to show you where discipline breaks down.

The complete scored assessment is available at **www.whyaifails.com**.

The next chapter addresses what happens when pilots succeed: scaling from pilot to production. But before we get there, kill your zombies. Until you establish pilot discipline, nothing else matters—you'll just find more sophisticated ways to waste resources.

Capability without discipline leads to sophisticated failure.

Chapter Eight

Scale Strategy—From Pilot to Production

The pilot succeeded brilliantly. Eight weeks, all success criteria exceeded, business case validated. The procurement optimization model reduced costs by 14% in the pilot population. Executives were thrilled. The project team celebrated. The CIO announced plans to scale immediately.

Six months later, the initiative was stalled. The model ran in production for forty-seven users out of a target population of 2,400. User adoption remained below 12%. Support tickets overwhelmed the help desk. The data engineering team spent 60% of their time troubleshooting production issues rather than building new capabilities. The CFO questioned whether to continue funding.

What happened? The pilot proved the technology worked. Why did scaling fail?

Because pilot success and production readiness are fundamentally different problems. Organizations assume pilot success predicts production success. They underestimate the infrastructure, change management, and support model differences between serving fifty users and serving 2,500. They rush deployment and neglect adoption, then wonder why usage remains anemic.

Scale strategy—the fifth pillar—is where disciplined execution meets organizational transformation. You've established strategic clarity, aligned leadership, built capability, and proven your pilot works. Now comes the hardest transition: converting experimental success into production value at scale.

The Scaling Chasm

The gap between pilot success and production deployment looks small on paper. In practice, it's a chasm that swallows resources, credibility, and careers. Even among pilots that demonstrate technical viability, the majority never achieve production-scale adoption.

Here's why good pilots fail at scale:

The Infrastructure Illusion

Pilots run on prototype infrastructure designed for experimentation, not production operations. Small data volumes. Simplified integrations. Manual workarounds. Tolerant users who forgive performance issues.

Production demands different foundations entirely. Real data volumes that stress systems. Full integration with enterprise architecture. Automated processes that run without intervention. Users who expect reliability, not patience.

Organizations discover this gap after launch. The pilot ran smoothly on 50,000 records processed weekly. Production needs to handle two million records daily. The pilot accessed a clean data subset. Production must ingest messy data from forty-seven source systems. The pilot used a prototype API. Production requires enterprise-grade security, monitoring, and disaster recovery.

Rebuilding infrastructure post-launch adds four to six months most organizations never budgeted. During this period, the "production" system limps along with pilot-grade capability serving production-scale expectations. User frustration builds. Support costs spike. Executives question the investment.

Industry experience confirms the pattern: organizations that scale on pilot infrastructure face two to three times higher support costs and months of additional time-to-adoption compared to those that build production-grade systems from the start.

> **RED FLAG: The Pilot-Production Chasm**
> Your scaling initiative is heading for failure if:
> - Production infrastructure is "same as pilot, just bigger"
> - Support model is "add more people to help desk"
> - Training is "send documentation and videos"
> - Change management is "announce at town hall"
> - Timeline assumes "flip the switch" deployment
> - Budget doesn't triple for production versus pilot
> - Executive sponsor thinks "the hard part is done"
>
> **Action:** Build production readiness assessment using framework below. Don't proceed to scale until all dimensions score 3+.

The Support Model Gap

Pilots survive with minimal support because pilot users tolerate ambiguity. They understand they're testing experimental technology. They're willing to troubleshoot. They provide detailed feedback. They forgive failures.

Production users expect systems to work. They want immediate answers when things break. They have jobs to do that don't include debugging your AI. When the system fails, they need help now—not a ticket response in forty-eight hours.

Organizations scale the technology but not the support model. Twenty users shared a single point of contact who knew the system intimately. Two thousand users need a tiered support structure with documentation, training resources, and escalation processes. The pilot ran during business hours. Production runs 24/7.

The mismatch creates predictable chaos. Help desk tickets overwhelm support teams unfamiliar with the AI system. Users grow frustrated and stop using it. Support costs explode beyond budget. The project team spends all their time firefighting instead of improving the system.

> **RED FLAG: The Change Management Afterthought**
> You planned deployment but not adoption, so your AI system sits unused while people work around it.
>
> Watch for these warning signs:
>
> - Technical deployment is on schedule but no user training plan exists
>
> - Change management was added in the last month before launch
>
> - End users learned about the new system from IT, not their managers

- Adoption metrics weren't defined before deployment

Action: Integrate change management from day one of scale planning. Technical deployment and organizational adoption must advance in parallel. A system nobody uses isn't a deployment success—it's an expensive shelf ornament.

The Change Management Void

The third gap cuts deepest. Pilots bypass organizational change management entirely.

Pilot users volunteer. They're early adopters who want new technology. They adapt their workflows to accommodate the system. They're motivated to make it succeed.

Production users are assigned. Many are skeptical. Most have established workflows they're comfortable with. They need the AI to adapt to them, not vice versa. They don't care about innovation—they care about whether this helps them do their jobs better.

Organizations treat scaling as deployment instead of transformation. They announce availability and expect adoption. No workflow redesign. No comprehensive training. No champions in each department. No communication strategy beyond a launch email.

Then they're baffled when usage stalls at 15%. The technology works. Why aren't people using it?

Because you deployed a system, not a transformation. Production success requires changing how thousands of people work. That demands change management infrastructure most AI teams never build.

The scaling chasm exists because organizations confuse technical deployment with organizational adoption. They think scaling means bigger servers and more users. It means transformation capability—and most organizations lack the discipline to build it.

> **RED FLAG: The Operations Orphan**
> Development team moved on to the next pilot and no one owns production support—your asset is becoming a liability.
> Watch for these warning signs:
> - No dedicated team owns the system post-deployment
> - Bug reports go to developers who've moved to other projects
> - System monitoring is reactive (wait for complaints) not proactive
> - Knowledge of how the system works lives in one person's head
>
> **Action:** Establish production ownership before deployment begins. Define SLAs, escalation paths, and dedicated support capacity. The moment a system goes to production without an owner, the decay clock starts.

The Scale Strategy Framework

Effective scaling isn't complicated. It requires discipline to build four capabilities before deployment, not after problems emerge.

Production Readiness Assessment

Before scaling any pilot, evaluate production readiness across six dimensions: technical infrastructure, process integration, change management readiness, support model, stakeholder coalition, and value case strength. Each dimension requires explicit preparation. Skipping any dimension predicts scaling failure.

Technical infrastructure determines whether your systems can handle production volume—fifty times the pilot data, enterprise integration, production-grade security, and real-time monitoring. Organizations scaling on pilot infrastructure pay later with outages, security incidents, and performance degradation.

Process integration measures how completely the AI system connects with organizational processes: approvals, compliance reviews, data governance, security assessments, vendor management. The pilot likely bypassed many. Production cannot. Less than 60% process integration predicts deployment delays and compliance issues.

Change management readiness separates planned transformation from announced deployment. Organizations without comprehensive change management achieve less than 25% user adoption after six months.

Support model readiness is consistently underestimated. Support scales nonlinearly—twenty users need a single contact, two thousand need 24/7 infrastructure. Support typically exceeds initial development cost two to three times over three years.

Stakeholder coalition must span the organization: IT operations, compliance, training, budget owners, affected departments. Building this coalition during pilots is easier than building it during a production crisis.

Value case strength provides the insurance against scaling failure. When you prove production value before deployment, stakeholder resistance evaporates.

The complete Production Readiness Assessment with scoring rubric and interpretation guide is available at **www.whyaifails.com**.

> **RED FLAG: The Performance Surprise**
> Organizations accumulate infrastructure debt by scaling pilots without production rebuilding. The pattern:
> - Pilot works well on development systems
> - Executive pressure to deploy quickly
> - Production deployment on "enhanced" pilot infrastructure
> - Issues emerge under production load—too late to redesign
> - Four-to-six-month recovery period with degraded performance and high support costs
> - Meanwhile competitors continue advancing
>
> **Action:** If you're answering "we'll fix it in production," you're already three months into a disaster. Rebuild for production before you deploy.

Wave Deployment Strategy

Rushing from pilot to full production is a common failure pattern. Disciplined organizations deploy progressively—starting with early adopters and learning with each wave.

This approach feels slow. It isn't. Progressive deployment accelerates total time-to-value because each wave learns and improves. An impatient big-bang deployment crashes, gets rolled back, and demands a complete restart—adding three months.

Wave 1: Enthusiasts

Deploy first to your most enthusiastic users—the volunteers who wanted the pilot to succeed. They tolerate issues, provide detailed feedback, and champion the system to skeptics.

Target first wave: ten to twenty percent of production population. Timeline: four to six weeks.

Success criteria for Wave 1: 70%+ adoption among first wave users, system stability, support model functioning, clear user feedback on improvements.

Learn from Wave 1: What worked? What surprised you? What do future waves need differently?

Wave 2: Early Adopters

Wave 2 targets pragmatists—users who see value in the system and adopt when it's proven. They're less tolerant of issues than Wave 1, so address all critical issues before deployment.

Target second wave: Additional thirty to forty percent of production population. Timeline: six to eight weeks.

Success criteria for Wave 2: 60%+ adoption among Wave 2 users, system stability sustained, support model scaling effectively, business case metrics tracking to projections.

Critical insight for Wave 2: This is where you learn whether your support model scales. If support is overwhelmed in Wave 2, fix it before Wave 3. Scaling broken support to your entire population is catastrophic.

Wave 3: Mainstream

Wave 3 targets the broader population—users who'll adopt once others validate the system. By this phase, you have production proof points, process validation, and support model maturity.

Target third wave: Remaining forty to fifty percent of production population. Timeline: eight to twelve weeks.

Success criteria for Wave 3: 50%+ adoption among Wave 3 users, sustained system reliability, value metrics reaching business case projections, support model demonstrating sustainability.

Wave Management Discipline

Key principles across all waves:

Define go/no-go criteria before each wave. What performance or adoption metrics must be met before advancing? Make those criteria explicit, then enforce them ruthlessly. "We'll make it work" is not a go/no-go criterion. "70% adoption with 95% system uptime" is.

Adapt between waves. If Wave 1 reveals inadequate training, improve it before Wave 2. If Wave 1 exposes an understaffed support model, add capacity before Wave 2. Scaling broken processes guarantees disaster.

Communicate wave results transparently. Share what worked and what needs improvement. Transparency demonstrates learning and builds confidence that issues are being addressed.

Pace deployment to support capacity. The speed of wave deployment is governed by support capacity, not technical readiness. A system technically ready for 5,000 users but supported for 100 will fail regardless of technical excellence.

RED FLAG: The Big Bang Fantasy
Organizations often compress or skip wave discipline under executive pressure. "We don't have time for three waves—let's deploy to everyone in one month."
This thinking typically leads to:

> - Week 1: Enthusiastic launch
> - Weeks 2–3: Issues emerge
> - Week 4: Support overwhelmed
> - Week 5: Public failures
> - Weeks 6–8: Emergency fixes
> - Week 9+: Gradual user adoption once credibility is restored
>
> Total time to meaningful adoption: twelve-plus weeks instead of nine to ten weeks with disciplined waves. Same timeline, worse credibility damage.
>
> **Action:** Resist the pressure to skip waves. Disciplined progressive deployment reaches full adoption faster than big-bang launches that crash and require recovery.

Common Obstacles and Solutions

Production scaling inevitably hits obstacles. These three occur most frequently:

Obstacle 1: The Budget Surprise

Manifestation: Pilot approved but production budget not secured. Sticker shock when seeing full production costs. Pressure to "do production with pilot budget." Competition with other initiatives for resources.

Root Causes: Production costs not included in original business case. Disconnect between pilot approval and production commitment. Underestimation of production infrastructure and support requirements.

Solutions: Include production costs in the pilot business case from the start. Secure conditional production budget at pilot approval. Quantify the opportunity cost of not scaling a successful pilot. Present production as investment, not expense. Enlist executive sponsorship for budget advocacy.

Prevention: Business case always includes full production lifecycle costs. Pilot approval includes production budget commitment. Regular stakeholder updates prevent surprise at production costs.

Obstacle 2: IT Operations Resistance

Manifestation: Operations team objects to production handoff. Concerns about supportability and reliability. Demands for extensive documentation and process compliance. Delays in production deployment approvals.

Root Causes: Operations not engaged during pilot development. Concerns about inheriting unfamiliar technology. Legitimate gaps in production readiness. Unclear support model and responsibilities. Past experience with failed handoffs.

Solutions: Engage the operations team from pilot start, not at production. Include operations requirements in pilot design. Provide comprehensive documentation and knowledge transfer. Define a clear support model with explicit responsibilities. Run a trial support period before full handoff. Incorporate operations input on production readiness criteria.

Prevention: Operations represented in pilot governance from day one. Production readiness criteria co-defined with operations. Pilot built with operations requirements in mind.

Obstacle 3: Technical Performance Issues at Scale

Manifestation: System performed well in pilot, degrades in production. Infrastructure capacity insufficient for actual usage.

Integration issues emerge under real-world conditions. Reliability problems affecting user trust.

Root Causes: Pilot used development infrastructure with shortcuts. Failed to test at realistic production scale. Integration testing with controlled data, not production complexity. Assumptions about usage patterns proved incorrect.

Solutions: Optimize performance and expand capacity immediately. Invest in infrastructure to handle actual scale. Load-test with realistic usage patterns. Refine integrations with production data and conditions. Roll back temporarily to a smaller user base if necessary.

Prevention: Pilot built on production-equivalent infrastructure. Testing at ten times pilot volume before production. Production data integration testing during pilot. Capacity planning based on pessimistic assumptions.

The Truth About Scale Strategy

Scaling is where AI transformation lives or dies. Brilliant pilots mean nothing if they never escape the lab.

Scale requires speed—moving from pilot success to production before momentum fades. It requires discipline—following progressive rollout even when pressure mounts to move faster. It requires investment—committing production resources that exceed pilot spending. It requires patience—accepting that scale takes six to nine months even with strong execution. It requires humility—learning from each deployment wave and adapting your approach.

Most organizations fail at scale because they treat it as a deployment problem rather than a change management challenge. They underinvest in production transition relative to pilot spending. They skip progressive rollout. They never build the coalition necessary for production support. They celebrate pilot success without demanding production results.

Organizations that master scaling achieve far higher production success rates. They capture the majority of projected business case value. They build momentum that accelerates future scaling efforts. They develop organizational muscle that compounds over time. They transform AI from experiment to competitive advantage.

The question isn't whether your pilots can succeed—many pilots succeed. The question is whether you can scale those successes into production systems that actually transform your business. Master this pillar or accept that your AI investments will remain science projects.

Scaling without guardrails creates liability, not assets. The next pillar, Risk Management, determines whether your scaled systems become strategic advantages or compliance nightmares.

Chapter Nine

Risk Management— Building Guardrails That Enable

"We're going to pause the AI implementation."

The team was three months into a major customer-facing AI deployment when the Chief Risk Officer made this announcement. The system was working. Customers loved it. Business metrics exceeded projections.

"What's the problem?" the CIO asked.

"We discovered that the model occasionally generates responses that could be interpreted as financial advice. We're not licensed to provide financial advice. Legal says we need to review every potential regulatory implication before proceeding."

The next six months disappeared into regulatory review, documentation, and control implementation. The pause cost nearly $6 million in lost momentum, delayed revenue, remediation work, and competitive positioning—not to mention damaged credibility with stakeholders. All because the team hadn't addressed risk proactively.

This was avoidable. They knew they were in a regulated industry. They knew customers might ask financial questions. They should have anticipated this risk, designed appropriate guardrails, and secured regulatory approval before deployment.

Risk management—the sixth pillar—builds guardrails that enable rather than block AI adoption. It's not about eliminating risk (impossible) or blocking innovation (destructive). It's about understanding risks, implementing proportionate controls, and making informed decisions about acceptable risk levels.

> **RED FLAG: Deployment First, Safety Second**
> **Risk assessment happens** after the AI is built and business case approved, making it a rubber stamp, not an evaluation.
> - Risk review is the last step before deployment, not the first step of design
> - Risk team sees the system for the first time during pre-launch review
> - Business case was approved before anyone assessed risk implications
> - "We'll address risk concerns in the next phase" has been said more than once
>
> **Action:** Embed risk assessment into the earliest stages of initiative design. Risk management that starts after investment decisions are made is compliance theater. Real risk management shapes which investments get made.

The Risk Avoidance Trap

Most organizations approach AI risk in one of two dysfunctional ways.

Approach 1: Risk Ignorance

"We'll deal with risks if they become problems. Let's move fast and figure it out later."

This approach treats risk as an obstacle to innovation. It prioritizes speed over safety, excitement over evaluation. It works until it doesn't—and when risk materializes, the consequences are catastrophic. Regulatory violations with significant penalties. Data breaches that destroy customer trust. Model failures causing business damage. Reputational harm from AI mistakes. Legal liability from AI decisions.

Approach 2: Risk Paralysis

"We can't deploy AI until we've addressed every possible risk. Let's study this for another six months."

This approach treats all risks as unacceptable. It demands certainty impossible to achieve. Endless risk assessments that never conclude. Requirements for zero-risk guarantees. Process barriers that prevent experimentation. Competitive disadvantage from inaction.

Neither approach works. Risk ignorance creates ticking time bombs. Risk paralysis prevents value creation.

The Third Way: Risk-Informed Innovation

Build guardrails that enable safe experimentation within boundaries. Understand potential risks before deployment. Implement controls proportionate to risk levels. Monitor for risk indicators continuously. Adjust guardrails based on learning. Accept appropriate risk in pursuit of value.

When Guardrails Accelerate Progress

A financial services organization (a composite drawn from several regulated-industry deployments) deploying AI for loan underwriting faced a familiar obstacle. The compliance team's initial reaction was predictable: "We need twelve to eighteen months of review before any deployment."

Leadership took a different approach. They brought risk and compliance into the design process from day one. The team identified the real regulatory requirements versus perceived ones and built guardrails directly into the system architecture:

- **Explainability requirements**: Every AI recommendation included the three primary factors driving the decision, with clear audit trails showing how those factors were weighted.

- **Human oversight boundaries**: AI could recommend approval for standard cases within defined parameters. Anything outside those parameters required human review. The boundaries were based on regulatory requirements, not arbitrary caution.

- **Bias monitoring**: Automated testing ran daily across demographic groups, with explicit thresholds triggering investigation. Results went directly to the compliance team's dashboard.

- **Fallback mechanisms**: If the AI system experienced any anomaly, it seamlessly reverted to the traditional underwriting process. No customer ever experienced a system failure.

The result? The organization went from concept to production in four months instead of eighteen. The compliance team became advocates rather than obstacles because they had visibility and control. The guardrails weren't restrictions—they were enablers. They gave business leaders confidence to move fast because they knew the boundaries.

Three years later, that system has processed over $2 billion in loans with zero regulatory findings and 40% faster processing times. The guardrails didn't slow innovation. They accelerated it by removing the fear and uncertainty that paralyzes decision-making.

This is what effective risk management looks like: guardrails that expand the zone of acceptable innovation rather than restricting it.

The Three-Category Risk Framework

AI introduces risks across three categories. Understanding them enables proportionate risk management rather than a one-size-fits-all response.

Category 1: Operational Risks

What Can Break

AI systems can fail in ways that disrupt business operations. Model performance degrades as data patterns shift. AI failure triggers cascade failures in downstream systems. Data quality issues erode model accuracy. Infrastructure problems affect AI availability. Integration failures prevent AI from working with existing systems.

These are engineering risks. They require technical controls focused on reliability, monitoring, and resilience.

Example: A real-time inventory AI system fails during peak shopping season, causing cascade failures in order processing, fulfillment, and customer communications. The company loses $3 million in revenue over forty-eight hours before reverting to manual processes.

Core Control Strategy:

Build redundancy and monitoring. Track performance against baselines automatically, with alerts when degradation exceeds thresholds. Install circuit breakers that disable AI and revert to manual processes when error rates spike. Test regularly under load conditions that simulate real-world stress. Document rollback procedures that execute in minutes, not hours.

Category 2: Trust & Safety Risks

What Can Harm People

AI systems can make decisions that harm individuals or groups. Models amplify biases present in training data, systematically disadvantaging certain populations. Systems produce incorrect outputs with high confidence—the hallucination problem. Privacy violations occur when systems inadvertently expose sensitive information. Discriminatory outcomes emerge even from models that appear accurate on aggregate metrics.

These are ethical risks. They require controls focused on fairness, transparency, and accountability.

Example: A hiring AI system trained on ten years of historical hiring data systematically screens out qualified women candidates because historical hiring patterns favored men. The company faces regulatory investigation and $4.5 million in settlements before discovering the bias eighteen months after deployment.

Core Control Strategy:

Test for bias explicitly and continuously. Require fairness testing across demographic groups before any deployment, with explicit thresholds that must be met. Monitor outcomes across populations on an ongoing basis. Mandate human review for high-stakes decisions affecting individuals. Build explainability mechanisms that show why the AI made each decision. Conduct regular audits by parties independent of the development team.

> **RED FLAG: The Bias Assumption**
> **"Our data isn't biased"** is asserted without testing, making you legally and ethically liable when bias inevitably emerges.
> - No formal bias testing has been conducted on training data or model outputs
> - Team assumes proprietary data is inherently representative
> - Bias discussions focus on "our intent isn't biased" rather than measured outcomes
> - No ongoing monitoring for disparate impact across protected groups
> **Action:** Test for bias systematically, not assuming innocence. Every dataset reflects the biases of its collection process. Every model can amplify those biases. Measure outcomes across demographic groups and establish thresholds for acceptable variance. Intent doesn't prevent lawsuits—evidence does.

Category 3: Strategic Risks

What Can Destroy Value

AI investments can create long-term strategic liabilities rather than assets. Vendor lock-in breeds dependencies that increase costs and reduce optionality. Regulatory violations carry significant penalties and reputational damage. Competitive disadvantage emerges when AI initiatives consume resources without delivering value. Technical debt accumulates as systems become unmaintainable. Knowledge drains away when external vendors build everything and internal teams learn nothing.

These are business risks. They require controls focused on governance, capability building, and strategic alignment.

Example: An organization invests $9 million over three years in vendor-built AI systems for customer service, supply chain, and marketing. When business priorities shift, they discover they cannot modify any system without the vendor. Annual maintenance costs exceed $2 million, and they possess zero internal capability to adapt or extend what they've built. The AI investments became liabilities.

Core Control Strategy:

Retain strategic options. Avoid vendor lock-in through multi-vendor strategies or open-source alternatives. Build internal capability rather than outsourcing everything. Maintain a portfolio view of AI investments as assets or liabilities. Invest in internal talent development. Conduct regular strategic reviews of major AI investments. Establish clear escalation when strategic risks emerge.

The Governance Shift: From Gatekeepers to Enablers

Most organizations structure AI governance around risk avoidance: risk and compliance functions serve as gatekeepers that approve or reject initiatives. Risk becomes synonymous with "no." Innovation and risk operate as adversaries.

A better approach treats risk management as an enabling function. Risk expertise participates in design, helping teams build confidence through informed control decisions. Business, technology, and risk functions work as partners with a shared goal: move fast while managing risk appropriately.

Five questions that drive collaborative risk management:

1. **What could go wrong?** Identify and categorize potential risks across the three categories.

2. **What controls matter most?** Focus control effort on risks that could cause material harm. Don't waste effort on theoretical risks.

3. **How do we know if controls work?** Design monitoring systems that detect risks materializing, not just compliance documentation.

4. **Who decides?** Clear decision authority and accountability. Who can approve deployment? Who escalates when problems emerge?

5. **How do we learn?** Every incident becomes a learning opportunity. Blameless post-mortems focused on improving processes.

The shift from gatekeeper to enabler requires leadership commitment and cultural change around risk. It demands transparency about risks and honest conversations about acceptable risk levels. But the payoff is substantial: organizations that master this shift innovate faster while managing risk more effectively.

Five Failure Patterns in AI Risk Management

Most organizations stumble on risk management through the same predictable patterns. Recognizing them is the first step to avoiding them.

Failure 1: Process Theater Over Risk Reduction

Symptom: Elaborate risk assessment processes that produce thick documentation but don't reduce risk. "We checked the box, now we can deploy."

Root Cause: Risk management treated as compliance obligation rather than operational capability.

Consequence: Bureaucratic overhead that slows innovation without making systems safer.

Solution: Test control effectiveness, not just existence. Measure risk reduction, not process completion. Reward teams that find and fix problems, not those that produce perfect documentation.

> **RED FLAG: The Compliance Checkbox**
> **Your risk documentation** is comprehensive but controls are never tested, making you documented but not protected.
> - Risk register is complete and up-to-date but controls haven't been validated
> - Audit found documentation excellent but couldn't verify control effectiveness
> - Team can describe risk mitigation plans but hasn't tested them
> - Risk management is a document exercise, not an operational practice
> **Action:** Test every control. Risk documentation without validation is a filing exercise. Schedule regular control testing—

quarterly at minimum—and treat failed tests as urgent findings, not administrative inconveniences.

Failure 2: The Risk Department Owns Risk

Symptom: Business and IT teams abdicate risk responsibility to risk/compliance team. "That's their job to worry about."

Root Cause: Risk management seen as compliance function rather than everyone's responsibility.

Consequence: Risks identified too late. Controls don't fit operational reality. Blame-shifting when issues arise.

Solution: Business and IT own risks. Risk team provides expertise and oversight but doesn't own operational risk management.

> **RED FLAG: The Risk Department Owns Risk**
> **Business teams delegate** risk management to compliance function, so risks are documented by people who don't understand operations.
> - Business owners view risk management as "compliance's job"
> - Risk assessments are written by people who've never used the system
> - Operational risks are documented in language that doesn't match how the system works
> - Risk mitigation plans exist on paper but operators don't know about them
>
> **Action:** Make risk ownership follow operational ownership. The people who build, deploy, and operate AI systems must own risk identification and mitigation. Compliance provides frameworks and oversight. Business provides context and accountability. Neither can do the other's job.

Failure 3: Risk Assessment After Deployment

Symptom: Risk assessments conducted after AI is deployed. Controls retrofitted onto existing systems.

Root Cause: Speed prioritized over safety. Risk treated as obstacle rather than enabler. "Easier to ask forgiveness than permission."

Consequence: Expensive retrofits. Deployed systems pulled back. Missed risks materialize with full impact.

Solution: Require risk assessment before pilot approval. Build controls into design from the start. Permit no deployment without explicit risk acceptance.

Failure 4: The Bias Blind Spot

Symptom: Focus on technical and security risks while ignoring fairness risks. Assume "we're not biased" without testing.

Root Cause: Discomfort with fairness topics. Lack of expertise in bias detection. Assumption that technical accuracy ensures fairness.

Consequence: Biased AI systems deployed into production, creating regulatory violations, reputational damage, and harm to individuals.

Solution: Mandatory bias testing before any deployment affecting individuals. Ongoing monitoring across demographic groups. Explicit fairness thresholds that must be maintained.

Failure 5: Static Risk Assessment

Symptom: Risk assessment conducted at project start, never updated. Risks treated as static rather than dynamic.

Root Cause: Risk assessment seen as gate to pass rather than ongoing practice.

Consequence: New risks materialize without warning. Controls become outdated. The risk environment changes while management stands still.

Solution: Conduct risk reviews at major milestones. Monitor for emerging risks. Update risk assessments when systems evolve. Foster a culture of ongoing risk awareness.

> **RED FLAG: The One-Time Assessment**
> **Risk was assessed** at project start but never updated despite system evolution and changing threats, making your controls obsolete.
> - Initial risk assessment is more than six months old with no updates
> - System has been modified multiple times since risk was last evaluated
> - New threat categories (regulatory changes, adversarial attacks) haven't been assessed
> - Risk documentation describes the system as it was designed, not as it currently operates
> **Action:** Treat risk assessment as a living process. Schedule formal reviews quarterly and trigger reassessment whenever the system changes materially, the regulatory environment shifts, or new threat categories emerge. Static risk management is an oxymoron.

The Risk Management Maturity Model

Organizations that master risk management share five characteristics:

1. Risk as Competitive Advantage

They view risk management as a capability that enables faster innovation, not bureaucracy that slows it. Their risk processes help them move faster than competitors who either ignore risk or freeze in the face of it.

2. Proportionate Controls

They apply rigorous controls to high-stakes decisions and lighter controls to low-stakes ones. They invest control effort where it matters most. The best defense isn't avoiding risk; it's positioning so that when threats materialize, you're already prepared to absorb and counter them.

3. Collaborative Culture

Risk, business, and technology functions work as partners, not adversaries. Risk expertise improves solution quality. Business and technology expertise makes controls practical and effective.

4. Continuous Learning

They treat every incident as a learning opportunity. They conduct blameless post-mortems focused on improving processes, not punishing people. They share lessons across the organization.

5. Strategic Focus

They distinguish between risks that threaten business value and risks that threaten compliance paperwork. They obsess over the former and dispatch the latter efficiently. They recognize that the biggest risk is often strategic—building the wrong capabilities or accumulating liabilities disguised as assets.

The Simple Assessment

Evaluate your risk management capability:

Strong Risk Management:

- Risk assessments completed before pilot approval
- Controls built into system design, not retrofitted
- Regular bias testing for systems affecting individuals
- Monitoring systems that detect problems before users do
- Risk and business functions working as partners
- Clear escalation paths when issues emerge
- Documented risk acceptance for residual risks
- Portfolio view of whether AI builds assets or liabilities

Weak Risk Management:

- Risk assessments after deployment or not at all
- Controls added when problems occur
- No systematic bias testing
- Learn about problems from user complaints
- Risk functions working in isolation as gatekeepers
- Unclear accountability when issues arise
- Implicit rather than explicit risk acceptance
- No portfolio view of strategic risk

The difference between strong and weak isn't the presence of risk—both organizations face similar risks. The difference is whether risks are identified, evaluated, and managed proactively or discovered through expensive failures.

The Truth About Risk Management

Risk management isn't about eliminating risk. It's about understanding risk well enough to innovate responsibly.

The question isn't whether to manage AI risk—it's whether you manage it proactively or reactively. Organizations that master proactive risk management innovate faster, recover from incidents quickly, and earn the trust of regulators and stakeholders. Those that fail either block innovation through excessive caution or suffer catastrophic failures that destroy value and trust.

THE BOTTOM LINE

What Matters:
Risk management isn't about blocking innovation—it's about
enabling it responsibly. Organizations that build collaborative
guardrails innovate faster than those that skip governance
entirely or bury it in compliance bureaucracy.

Track This:
Percentage of AI initiatives with documented risk assessments
covering operational, trust and safety, and strategic risk
categories. Measure time from risk identification to mitigation
action. Monitor the ratio of proactive risk management
activities to reactive incident responses.

Do This:
Within thirty days, audit every production AI system for
documented risk ownership and escalation paths. Within sixty
days, establish a collaborative governance framework that
includes technical, business, legal, and ethics perspectives.
Within ninety days, implement continuous risk monitoring
with clear thresholds and response protocols.

Scaled systems in production don't maintain themselves—they
decay. The next pillar addresses how organizations build the
disciplines that keep AI investments improving long after launch
day.

Chapter Ten

Continuous Evolution—The Learning Discipline

Around 2020, an organization celebrated a breakthrough. Their customer service chatbot was sophisticated for its time—natural language understanding, context awareness, integration with enterprise systems. Launch metrics exceeded expectations: 65% resolution rate, 4.2 out of 5.0 satisfaction scores, 30% reduction in call center volume. The ROI calculation showed payback in eighteen months. Leadership declared victory. The AI team moved to their next project.

By 2023, the CIO had a problem. "Our chatbot is dying," he told his leadership team. "Resolution rates dropped to 45%. Satisfaction is 3.1. Call center volume is back up. Customers complain it doesn't understand them anymore."

A review of the system confirmed the technology still worked. The infrastructure ran fine. The problem wasn't technical failure. It was organizational abandonment.

Everything had changed. The company had launched three new products the chatbot knew nothing about. They reorganized customer service twice—new processes, new terminology. Customer expectations evolved with the market. Return policies changed. Their knowledge base quadrupled. But the AI still answered based on 2019 data, processes, and language.

The original team had moved on. Documentation was sparse. The vendor they worked with got acquired. Nobody left understood how it worked or how to evolve it. Leadership evaluated whether to rebuild from scratch or shut it down.

The system cost $2.3 million to build. It generated strong value for eighteen months. Then it decayed—slowly at first, then rapidly—until it became more liability than asset. Total lifecycle value: roughly $1.5 million. Net loss: $800,000, plus three years of degrading customer experience.

This is the silent death of AI systems. They don't crash spectacularly. They rot gradually—becoming less relevant, less effective, less valuable with each passing month. Organizations that fail to embed continuous evolution disciplines watch their AI investments decay into liabilities.

The seventh pillar—Continuous Evolution—determines whether AI systems compound advantage over years or quietly rot into technical debt that eventually demands replacement.

The Decay Pattern

AI systems decay predictably. This pattern repeats across dozens of organizations. Understanding it is the first step toward prevention.

Phase 1: Peak Performance (Months 0–6)

The system launches. Everything is optimized for current reality. Training data is fresh. Processes align with operations.

The team that built it maintains intimate knowledge. Edge cases get quick fixes. Performance metrics meet or exceed targets.

This is the honeymoon period. The system works because it was designed for this exact moment.

Phase 2: Subtle Degradation (Months 6–18)

Small misalignments emerge. New products launch that the system doesn't recognize. Processes evolve but the AI doesn't. Team members rotate to new projects. Edge case response slows. Performance metrics drift downward but remain acceptable.

This is the dangerous phase. Problems are real but not urgent. Decay is underway but isn't visible enough to demand attention.

Phase 3: Obvious Decline (Months 18–36)

Performance degradation becomes visible. Users complain. Workarounds proliferate. Business value erodes noticeably. The gap between system capability and organizational reality grows too large to ignore.

This is the crisis phase. The system needs major updates but the knowledge required has dispersed. Fixing it requires archaeology—rediscovering how it works, why decisions were made, what dependencies exist.

Phase 4: Zombie Status (Months 36+)

The system exists but delivers minimal value. It's maintained minimally because turning it off seems harder than keeping it running. Resources flow to new initiatives rather than resurrection. Eventually someone asks whether to rebuild or abandon it.

This is the endpoint of organizational neglect. The investment becomes a liability consuming resources while delivering declining returns.

The pattern is remarkably consistent. Without deliberate evolution discipline, every system moves through these phases on a predictable timeline. The world changes. The AI doesn't. Eventually it becomes more liability than asset.

> **RED FLAG: The Immortal System Illusion**
> Your organization treats deployed AI as permanent infrastructure rather than evolving capability:
> - Systems launch with no scheduled review or retraining cadence
> - Nobody monitors model drift or performance degradation
> - The deployment budget included zero allocation for ongoing evolution
> - Leadership treats "it's working" as the end state rather than the starting point
>
> **Action:** Establish an evolution plan for every deployed system before launch. Define retraining triggers, performance thresholds, and review cadence. Systems without evolution plans are liabilities on a countdown.

Why Decay Happens

Decay isn't inevitable—it's organizational. Three forces drive AI system degradation when evolution discipline is absent.

Force 1: Reality Shift

The world changes continuously. Customer expectations evolve. Products change. Processes adapt. Markets shift. Regulations update. Competitors innovate. Technology advances.

AI systems reflect the reality they were trained on. When that reality shifts and the system doesn't adapt, the gap widens. A customer service chatbot trained on 2019 data struggles with 2022 products. A fraud detection model built before the pandemic misses new fraud patterns. A pricing algorithm optimized for low-inflation economics makes poor decisions in high-inflation environments.

The shift is gradual—invisible day to day but dramatic year over year. By the time organizations notice performance degradation, the system requires major surgery rather than incremental evolution.

Force 2: Knowledge Dispersion

The people who built the system move on. They join other projects, get promoted, leave the company. Their deep understanding—why certain architectural choices were made, which edge cases matter, how components interact—leaves with them.

Documentation helps but never captures everything. Tacit knowledge—the intuition developed through building and refining the system—resists transfer. New team members inherit a black box. They can operate it but don't understand it well enough to evolve it confidently.

When problems emerge, the knowledge required to fix them no longer exists in the organization. Response time slows. Solutions become patches rather than proper fixes. The system becomes increasingly brittle.

RED FLAG: Launch Amnesia
The team that built it has moved on and tribal knowledge left with them:

- The original development team has been reassigned or has left the company
- Documentation is incomplete or outdated
- Operations inherited an undocumented system they can operate but cannot evolve
- When problems emerge, response time doubles because institutional knowledge is gone

Action: Require knowledge transfer and documentation handoff as a deployment gate. No system goes to production until operations can independently troubleshoot, retrain, and evolve it.

Force 3: Resource Reallocation

Leadership attention gravitates toward new initiatives. New AI projects are exciting—they promise fresh value, attract executive attention, demonstrate progress. Existing systems are mature—they work, they're boring, they don't need attention.

Resource allocation follows attention. Budgets fund new builds, not system evolution. Talented people want new challenges, not maintenance duty. Investment in keeping systems current competes with investment in new capabilities—and new almost always wins.

The logic seems sound: why spend on maintenance when you could invest in growth? But neglect creates technical debt. Systems decay. Eventually the debt demands payment—expensive rehabilitation or complete replacement.

Organizations that don't balance new builds with sustained evolution pay more overall. Regular evolution costs less than periodic replacement. But the investment patterns look different. Evolution is steady, unglamorous spending. Replacement is dramatic, budget-consuming crisis.

The resource allocation question is unavoidable: fund new initiatives while existing systems decay, or balance new builds with sustained evolution? Most organizations choose new initiatives—they're exciting, they attract executive attention, they show action. The disciplined minority balance both— because they understand that systems without evolution become liabilities demanding expensive replacement.

Building Organizations vs. Learning Organizations

The distinction between building and learning organizations explains why some AI portfolios compound value while others accumulate technical debt.

Building organizations deploy AI systems successfully. They have capable teams, sound methodologies, and effective execution. They launch on time and on budget. They meet initial success criteria. They celebrate launches and move to the next project.

But building organizations don't capture learning systematically. Knowledge stays with individuals. Each project reinvents approaches. Mistakes repeat across initiatives. Improvement happens sporadically through individual insight, not institutional discipline. Systems launch successfully but decay gradually.

Learning organizations do everything building organizations do—and add systematic learning disciplines. They capture knowledge from every initiative. They document patterns that work and failures to avoid. They transfer learning across teams. They improve processes continuously. They build capability that compounds over time.

Learning organizations don't just deploy AI—they build organizational capacity to deploy AI with increasing effectiveness. Each initiative launches faster, costs less, and performs better than the last. Knowledge accumulates. Capability compounds. Systems evolve continuously rather than decay.

The difference manifests in four core capabilities:

Capability 1: Systematic Knowledge Capture

Learning organizations treat every deployment as a learning opportunity. They conduct structured retrospectives: What worked? What didn't? What would we do differently? What patterns should we codify?

Insights get documented in accessible formats. Pattern libraries capture reusable approaches. Failure mode databases prevent repeated mistakes. Best practice documentation accelerates future initiatives. Organizational memory grows systematically.

Building organizations conduct retrospectives occasionally—but inconsistently, without structured formats, and rarely in reusable ways. Learning evaporates when individuals leave.

Capability 2: Institutional Memory Systems

Learning organizations create systems that ensure knowledge survives personnel changes. Documentation standards make systems understandable to new team members. Knowledge transfer protocols accompany role transitions. Critical systems have redundant expertise—never a single point of knowledge failure. Pattern libraries and decision records preserve institutional wisdom.

Building organizations rely on individual knowledge. When key people leave, understanding leaves with them. New team members face steep learning curves rediscovering tribal knowledge. The organization pays repeatedly for the same lessons.

Capability 3: Rapid Iteration Capability

Learning organizations build infrastructure that enables frequent, low-risk system updates. Automated testing catches regressions. Continuous integration pipelines accelerate deployment. Monitoring detects drift early. Feedback loops channel real-world performance into improvement cycles.

This infrastructure makes evolution affordable and routine. Small, frequent updates maintain system relevance without major overhauls. The organization adapts systems as reality shifts.

Building organizations treat updates as major undertakings—expensive, risky, infrequent. Systems go months or years between meaningful improvements. By the time updates happen, multiple issues have accumulated, making changes more complex and risky.

Capability 4: Evolution-Ready Culture

Learning organizations cultivate norms that support continuous improvement. They celebrate learning from failures, not just successes. They reward teams that evolve existing systems, not just those building new ones. They allocate resources to evolution explicitly. They treat AI systems as living capabilities requiring ongoing care, not finished products.

Building organizations have a culture that values launches. Teams want new projects, not maintenance work. Evolution budgets compete with new-build budgets—and lose. Leadership attention gravitates to launches, not improvements. The cultural message is clear: success means shipping, not evolving.

These four capabilities reinforce each other. Knowledge capture feeds institutional memory. Memory enables rapid iteration. Iteration depends on a culture that values evolution. All four are necessary. Without systematic knowledge capture, learning evaporates. Without institutional memory, capability vanishes. Without iteration infrastructure, insights never become improvements. Without evolution-ready culture, the other three atrophy.

The Compound Advantage Equation

Learning organizations compound advantage over time in ways building organizations cannot.

The compounding manifests across three dimensions:

Efficiency Compounds: Each AI initiative should be faster and cheaper than the previous because you're reusing platform components, applying learned patterns, leveraging experienced teams, and avoiding past mistakes.

Consider a target trajectory: Year 1 initiative takes twelve months and costs $1 million. Year 2: eight months, $600,000. Year 3: four months, $300,000. Year 4: two months, $150,000.

The cumulative efficiency gain over four years can reach six to ten times. Organizations not seeing this pattern aren't building capability—they're accumulating point solutions.

Capability Compounds: Each initiative builds organizational expertise that enables more sophisticated future work. Year 1: learn AI deployment basics. Year 2: develop domain expertise. Year 3: create institutional processes. Year 4: achieve mastery enabling sophisticated applications.

The cumulative capability gain enables initiatives that weren't possible initially. Early investments fund learning for advanced later work.

Value Compounds: AI capabilities build on each other, creating integrated value greater than the sum of parts. Year 1: point solutions delivering individual value. Year 2: connected capabilities delivering combined value. Year 3: an integrated AI portfolio with network effects. Year 4: AI-native operations creating exponential value.

When customer service AI informs sales prioritization, which influences inventory optimization, which shapes supply chain decisions, the integrated value far exceeds what individual components deliver alone.

Small improvements in any dimension compound powerfully over time. A 20% annual improvement doubles performance in four years, triples it in six, and quintuples it in nine.

Organizations focused on compounding build sustainable advantage. Organizations optimizing each project independently accumulate linear value while competitors compound exponential returns.

AI maturity isn't measured by how many models you've deployed—it's measured by depth of organizational capability. The organization that executes fundamentals with precision, speed, and adaptability outperforms the one with a longer list of deployed systems every time.

This insight transforms strategic thinking. The question shifts from "What's the ROI of this AI project?" to "How does this initiative build capability that compounds advantage over the next decade?"

Learning Organization Success: A Manufacturing Example

The following example is a composite drawn from documented cases across several manufacturing organizations, with financials representative of documented industry patterns.

A global manufacturing company deployed predictive maintenance AI in 2020. Initial results were strong: 40%

reduction in unplanned downtime, $8 million in annual savings. Most organizations would have declared success and moved on.

This organization committed to learning disciplines. Monthly retrospectives captured lessons from maintenance interventions. Quarterly business reviews analyzed effectiveness trends. A pattern library documented which predictions worked and which failed. Feedback loops connected maintenance outcomes back to model improvement.

Year 1 (2020): System performs well, generates $8 million in value, team documents forty-seven learned patterns.

Year 2 (2021): Team applies patterns to similar equipment, cutting deployment time 60%. System evolution improves prediction accuracy from 73% to 81%. Optimal sensor placement reduces false positives 40%. Annual value rises to $14 million.

Year 3 (2022): Expanded system covers 85% of critical equipment, up from 40%. A platform approach enables new-site deployment in six weeks versus nine months initially. Predictive accuracy reaches 87%. Integration with supply chain AI optimizes parts inventory. Annual value: $24 million.

Year 4 (2023): System predicts failures and optimal maintenance timing, reducing costs 20%. Institutional knowledge enables expansion to adjacent facilities with minimal customization. Annual value: $31 million.

Year 5 (2024): Competitors have similar predictive maintenance AI but lack evolution discipline. Their systems perform at 2020 baselines. This organization's system continues improving—89% accuracy, integrated with enterprise operations, enabling capabilities competitors cannot match. Annual value: $38 million.

Cumulative five-year value: $115 million. Initial investment: $14 million. Evolution investment: $15 million over five years. Net value: $86 million. A system that would have generated $45 million (five years at $9 million annually) instead generated more than 2.5 times that through sustained evolution.

The competitive gap is permanent. Competitors trying to catch up face the same learning curve this organization already climbed. Meanwhile, compounding continues to widen the advantage.

Building Learning Organization Capability: The Multi-Year Path

Creating learning organization capability requires sustained commitment. Most organizations underestimate the timeline. They want quick wins, but compound advantage takes years to manifest.

A realistic evolution timeline:

Year 1: Foundation Building

Establish basic infrastructure: implement a retrospective process for all projects with structured templates. Create an initial pattern library documenting lessons from recent initiatives. Set up system monitoring and alerting. Designate an evolution budget (20 to 30% of AI spending). Assign clear ownership for each production system's health.

Year 1 focuses on creating the essential infrastructure for learning. Don't expect dramatic improvements yet—you're building capability.

Year 2: Systematization

Deepen practices: implement comprehensive monitoring and alerting across all systems. Make quarterly strategic reviews standard practice with executive engagement. Establish formal knowledge transfer processes for role changes and promotions. Create a community of practice connecting AI practitioners across the organization. Conduct regular retrospectives with action items and ownership.

Year 2 transforms learning from ad hoc to systematic. Improvement velocity accelerates noticeably.

Year 3: Optimization

Refine and accelerate: develop predictive monitoring that identifies issues before they affect operations. Build a sophisticated pattern library guiding new initiatives from the start. Ensure organizational memory survives personnel changes through redundancy and documentation. Embed continuous learning throughout AI-enabled operations. Begin external engagement, sharing lessons and building reputation.

By Year 3, learning organization disciplines are embedded. The organization adapts continuously without heroic effort.

Ongoing: Sustainability

Maintain and evolve: refresh all AI systems regularly with current data and insights. Assess technology continuously and upgrade selectively. Adapt actively to market shifts and regulatory changes. Balance resource allocation between new builds and evolution. Celebrate and reward improvement.

This multi-year journey requires patience and persistence. Organizations that rush or skip phases fail. Those that commit to systematic capability building create compounding competitive advantage.

The key insight: building learning organization capability matters as much as building any specific AI system. Perhaps more—because it determines whether every AI investment compounds or decays over time.

The Evolution Imperative

AI systems are never "done." They require continuous care and evolution, or they decay into liabilities.

The distinction between building and learning organizations determines long-term AI success. Building organizations accumulate technical debt. Learning organizations compound advantage.

The choice is simple: Do you want your AI investments to compound advantage over years or decay into technical debt requiring periodic costly rebuilds?

Organizations that master continuous evolution maintain system effectiveness over years, not months. They build institutional knowledge that compounds. They adapt to market changes while preserving competitive advantage. They justify continued AI investment with sustained value delivery.

Organizations that fail at continuous evolution watch investments decay into liabilities. They repeat mistakes because learning isn't captured. They lose capability when people leave. They suffer declining returns from AI investments. They rebuild systems because maintenance was never designed in.

Continuous evolution requires discipline, investment, humility, memory, and culture. Most organizations struggle with at least three. All five are necessary. Without systematic knowledge capture, learning evaporates. Without institutional memory, capability vanishes. Without iteration infrastructure, insights never become improvements. Without evolution-ready culture, the other capabilities atrophy.

The seventh pillar determines whether AI transformation creates lasting competitive advantage or expensive technical debt. Master continuous evolution, or accept that your AI investments will decay, requiring periodic replacement at far greater cost than sustained evolution would have demanded.

Most organizations celebrate launch. The disciplined minority build learning systems that last.

The next chapter provides a systematic framework for evaluating every AI initiative's contribution to long-term competitive advantage—where discipline meets portfolio management.

PART III: PUTTING IT INTO PRACTICE

The Asset-Liability Assessment—Transforming Framework Into Action

From Framework to Assessment

Chapter 3 introduced the asset-liability lens—the principle that every AI investment either builds permanent organizational capability or accumulates expensive dependency. This chapter transforms that concept into a systematic assessment methodology: five scored tests that reveal whether your AI portfolio trends toward strategic asset or compounding liability.

The challenge is diagnostic. With a vendor pitch in front of you, budget pressure from the CFO, business stakeholders demanding results, and technology teams recommending approaches—how do you determine whether you're building an asset or accumulating a liability?

You need a systematic way to evaluate each initiative against objective criteria. You need scoring guidance that distinguishes genuine asset-building from vendor dependency dressed up as progress. And you need decision frameworks that connect assessment results to action.

This chapter delivers that methodology. The Asset-Liability Assessment translates the framework into a practical evaluation tool with five tests, each probing a dimension of asset-building capability. Organizations that succeed apply these tests rigorously. The rest skip assessment entirely, relying on vendor promises and internal optimism.

Each test includes five to seven questions. Your answers generate a score. The scores reveal patterns. The patterns inform decisions. The decisions determine whether you're building assets or accumulating liabilities.

Use this assessment before launching new initiatives to evaluate vendor proposals, build versus buy decisions, and resource allocation choices. Use it during execution to diagnose why pilots aren't scaling or why systems aren't delivering value. Use it quarterly to evaluate your entire AI portfolio— determining which initiatives deserve continued investment and which should be terminated immediately.

The five tests aren't complicated—but asking them demands discipline, answering them honestly demands courage, and acting on the results demands leadership commitment. That's why most organizations avoid rigorous assessment. It forces uncomfortable truths about initiatives already in flight.

> *Complete Assessment Available Online: This chapter presents the framework, sample questions, and scoring methodology for each test. The complete 34-question assessment with detailed scoring worksheets and automated calculators is available at whyaifails.com.*

The Five Tests in Detail

Test 1: Strategic Clarity Assessment

The first test determines whether your initiative serves a clear strategic purpose or merely responds to external pressure. Strategic clarity isn't about having a strategy document—it's about whether the initiative connects to specific business outcomes through a logical chain of cause and effect. The disciplined minority launch initiatives because they've identified how AI capabilities will improve specific business metrics. The majority launch because competitors are doing AI or because a vendor pitched a compelling demo.

This test probes strategic clarity through seven questions covering business problem articulation, metric definition, success criteria alignment, capability creation, scope boundaries, executive communication, and dependency assessment. The key diagnostic: Can you explain the business problem this initiative solves in one sentence without mentioning AI or technology? If you can't, you're not ready to invest. Each question scores 0 to 2 points for a maximum of 14 points.

Organizations scoring 12 or above have excellent strategic clarity—clear business purpose with defined success criteria. Those scoring 4 to 7 have weak clarity and high risk of becoming liabilities. Below 4 indicates no strategic clarity at all.

Common patterns: Organizations scoring high on business problem definition but low on capability questions typically have vendor-driven strategies. The reverse indicates technical teams building without business sponsorship. Low scores across all questions signal initiatives driven by politics, not strategy.

Test 2: Capability Readiness Assessment

The second test evaluates whether your organization has—or can develop—the capability to own this solution. Capability readiness isn't about current expertise. It's about whether you're structured to learn, whether you have the discipline to build knowledge, and whether your culture supports genuine capability development over vendor dependency.

Seven questions probe vendor independence, expertise development, budget allocation, IP ownership, knowledge transfer, system transparency, and post-launch evolution. The litmus test: If your current vendor disappeared tomorrow, could you continue operating this system? Maximum score: 14 points.

Organizations at 12 or above are structured to own solutions with lasting competitive advantage. At 4 to 7, capability is inadequate for ownership—either invest heavily or accept vendor dependency. Below 4 means complete vendor dependency guaranteed.

Common patterns: High technical talent with low knowledge-sharing scores signals capability concentration risk. Strong understanding with weak evolution plans means assets that will decay. Organizations scoring low across capability questions but convinced they're building assets are deceiving themselves.

Test 3: Execution Discipline Assessment

The third test evaluates whether your organization has the discipline to execute asset-building initiatives—or whether it gets distracted, changes direction, or accepts mediocre results. Most organizations lose discipline under pressure. The rare few who succeed maintain discipline precisely when pressure increases.

Six questions probe governance authority, success criteria enforcement, criteria stability, decision quality, scope discipline, and direction maintenance. The telling question: Are success criteria hard stops—would you kill this initiative if criteria aren't met? Maximum score: 12 points.

Organizations at 10 or above have excellent execution discipline. At 4 to 6, discipline is weak with risk of scope creep and direction drift. Below 4 means the initiative will be compromised by organizational pressure.

Common patterns: High criteria scores with low trade-off discipline means the team hasn't been tested yet—discipline shows under pressure, not in planning. Low scores across all dimensions indicate an environment too chaotic for asset-building.

Test 4: Risk Tolerance Assessment

The fourth test evaluates whether your organization can tolerate the risks inherent in asset-building or defaults to safer vendor dependency. Risk tolerance isn't recklessness—it's accepting calculated risks that enable capability building while managing catastrophic risks systematically.

Seven questions probe risk articulation, failure tolerance, exit criteria, risk allocation, track record, organizational stability, and risk governance. The key diagnostic: Is there a point at which you would stop this initiative and declare it a learning investment rather than a sunk cost? Maximum score: 14 points.

Organizations at 12 or above have excellent risk management and can proceed with confidence. At 4 to 7, risk tolerance is insufficient for asset-building—consider whether vendor services better match risk appetite. Below 4 indicates an environment unsuited to asset-building.

Common patterns: High risk awareness with low failure tolerance over-manages initiatives into mediocrity. Low awareness with high tolerance is luck, not skill.

Test 5: Evolution Capability Assessment

The fifth test evaluates whether your organization can evolve and improve this capability over time, or whether you're building a system destined to decay. Most organizations build disposable systems requiring rebuilds every two to three years. The disciplined few build systems that improve annually and compound over time.

Seven questions probe ongoing measurement, continuous improvement, learning capture, team continuity, degradation monitoring, technology evolution, and commitment horizon. The critical question: What's your commitment horizon—years or quarters? Maximum score: 14 points.

Organizations at 12 or above have systems designed to compound annually. At 4 to 7, systems will decay unless improvement culture strengthens. Below 4 means the system will require a complete rebuild within two to three years.

Common patterns: High measurement with low improvement scores indicates visibility into degradation but no resources to fix it. High learning with a low commitment horizon treats initiatives as exercises rather than lasting assets.

Applying the Assessment: Decision Framework

You've completed the five tests. You have scores for Strategic Clarity, Capability Readiness, Execution Discipline, Risk Tolerance, and Evolution Capability. Now what?

Individual test scores reveal specific strengths and vulnerabilities. The real power comes from combining scores across all five dimensions. Total score reveals trajectory. Patterns across tests reveal specific challenges. Both together inform the decisions that determine whether you build lasting capability or accumulate expensive liabilities.

Interpreting Total Scores

Sum your scores across all five tests. Maximum possible: 68 points.

58–68 points: STRONG ASSET TRAJECTORY

This initiative shows strong asset-building characteristics across all dimensions. Proceed with confidence. These are the initiatives that build lasting competitive advantage.

Recommended actions:

- Prioritize resources and leadership attention
- Protect from organizational turbulence
- Document approach for replication
- Use as template for future initiatives
- Invest in scaling when ready

Leadership message: "This is what right looks like. Protect it, learn from it, replicate it."

43–57 points: MODERATE ASSET POTENTIAL

This initiative shows asset potential but has meaningful gaps. Strengthen weak dimensions before scaling. Most organizations live in this range—decent foundations but incomplete execution.

Recommended actions:

- Identify the two to three lowest-scoring tests
- Develop specific improvement plans
- Set sixty-day timeline to address gaps
- Reassess before major resource commitment
- Consider whether gaps can be closed given organizational constraints

Leadership message: "This has potential but needs work. Fix specific weaknesses or accept this becomes liability."

28–42 points: NEUTRAL/HIGH RISK

This initiative has mixed characteristics—some asset qualities, some liability indicators. Proceeding means accepting significant risk of vendor dependency with limited capability building.

Recommended actions:

- Honest assessment: Can weaknesses be addressed?
- If yes: Pause, fix fundamentals, reassess
- If no: Be explicit this is vendor dependency, not capability building
- Consider whether vendor service model is appropriate
- Adjust expectations and budget accordingly

Leadership message: "This doesn't build meaningful capability. Either fix fundamentals or acknowledge it's a service purchase."

0–27 points: LIABILITY TRAJECTORY

This initiative has predominantly liability characteristics. Without major changes, it will consume resources, deepen vendor dependency, and deliver minimal lasting value. Strong candidate for termination.

Recommended actions:

- Consider termination seriously
- If continuing: Complete redesign required, not incremental fixes
- Set aggressive reassessment timeline (thirty days maximum)
- Communicate honestly about liability trajectory
- Redirect resources to higher-scoring initiatives

Leadership message: "This joins the 95%. Kill it or completely redesign it. Half-measures waste everyone's time."

Pattern Recognition Across Tests

Total score matters, but patterns across tests reveal specific challenges:

Pattern 1: Strong Strategy, Weak Capability (High Test 1, Low Test 2)

You know what you want but lack the ability to own it. This pattern indicates vendor dependency disguised as strategy. It often results from consultant-driven or vendor-driven planning.

Decision: Either invest heavily in capability building before proceeding, or acknowledge this will be a vendor service, not an internal asset. Pretending vendor dependency is capability building is expensive self-deception.

Pattern 2: Strong Capability, Weak Strategy (Low Test 1, High Test 2)

You have talent but no clear purpose. This pattern indicates technology-driven initiatives without business sponsorship—technical teams building interesting capabilities in a strategic vacuum.

Decision: Pause execution until strategy strengthens. Technical capability without business purpose produces impressive demos that deliver no value.

Pattern 3: Strong Strategy and Capability, Weak Execution (High Tests 1–2, Low Test 3)

You know what to do and can do it, but lack the discipline to execute. This pattern indicates governance and accountability problems, often rooted in a consensus culture unable to make hard decisions.

Decision: Fix governance before proceeding. Strategy and capability wasted without execution discipline. Appoint empowered leader, establish kill authority, set hard deadlines.

Pattern 4: Everything Strong Except Evolution (High Tests 1–4, Low Test 5)

You can launch successfully but systems will decay. This pattern reveals a "project" mindset rather than a "product" mindset, often driven by funding models that reward launches but starve operations.

Decision: Either fix evolution capabilities before launch (operations team, monitoring, budget) or acknowledge this is a disposable system requiring rebuild in two to three years. Factor rebuild costs into the ROI calculation.

Pattern 5: Consistently Mediocre (All Tests 5–7 Range)

Everything is "sort of okay" but nothing is excellent. This pattern signals organizational mediocrity—good enough to convince yourself to proceed, not good enough to succeed. It often results from political compromise.

Decision: Either commit to excellence in at least three of five dimensions or kill the initiative. Mediocrity across all dimensions guarantees mediocre results. Better to do fewer things excellently than many things adequately.

Build vs. Buy Decision Framework

Use assessment results to inform build versus buy decisions:

WHEN TO BUILD (Own the capability):

- Tests 1, 2, 5 score high (strategy, capability, evolution strong)
- Test 3 adequate or better (can execute with discipline)
- Strategic importance high
- Capability will be differentiating
- Long-term advantage matters more than short-term speed

WHEN TO BUY (Vendor service):

- Test 2 scores low and gap too large to close (capability lacking)
- Test 5 scores low with no intention to fix (no evolution capability)
- Commodity capability, not differentiating

- Time-to-market critical
- Acceptable to have vendor dependency

WHEN TO PARTNER (Hybrid model):

- Test 2 moderate with plan to build (capability developing)
- Tests 1, 3 strong (clear strategy, good execution)
- Vendor provides acceleration, not permanent crutch
- Knowledge transfer explicit in partnership
- Path to independence clear

Portfolio Decisions

Apply assessment across your entire AI portfolio to make portfolio-level decisions:

Portfolio Health Metrics:

- What percentage of initiatives score 58+ (strong assets)?
- What percentage score below 28 (liabilities)?
- Are scores improving or declining over time?
- Do patterns reveal organizational capabilities or gaps?

Portfolio Actions:

- Rank initiatives by total score
- Kill bottom 20 to 30% (liabilities consuming resources)
- Double down on top 20 to 30% (strong assets)
- Fix middle 40 to 60% or accept as vendor services
- Track portfolio trajectory quarterly

In healthy AI portfolios, 30% or more of initiatives in the strong asset range, with fewer than 20% in the liability range. Unhealthy portfolios show the inverse.

Case Study: Assessment in Action

The Situation

The following case study is a composite drawn from several healthcare organizations facing similar challenges. A $4.2 billion healthcare organization launched an AI initiative to improve patient scheduling efficiency—a problem costing an estimated $23 million annually through no-shows, double-bookings, and staff inefficiency. The CIO championed the initiative, secured $8 million in funding, and engaged a prominent AI vendor offering "proven healthcare scheduling optimization."

Six months in, the vendor presented a polished slide deck of technical metrics at a steering committee meeting while the COO stared at the ceiling. When the presentation ended, she asked one question: "Can anyone in this room explain how this system actually works?" No one could. The initiative was consuming resources while creating no lasting value. The vendor's system worked technically but failed to address the organization's specific workflow complexity. The team had learned only vendor-specific implementation skills. Post-launch evolution depended entirely on the vendor. Internal capability remained zero.

The CIO applied the Asset-Liability Assessment.

Assessment Results

Test 1: Strategic Clarity (8 points - MODERATE)

The business problem was clear: $23 million in efficiency losses. But success criteria had drifted. The business expected 15 to 20% efficiency improvement; the vendor's system delivered

8% technically, but organizational processes hadn't changed to capture even those gains.

Test 2: Capability Readiness (4 points - WEAK)

The team had learned vendor platform navigation but developed no independent capability. If the vendor relationship ended, the organization retained nothing. All evolution and maintenance depended on the vendor.

Test 3: Execution Discipline (6 points - WEAK)

Governance was consensus-driven rather than empowered. Scope expanded as stakeholders requested "just one more feature." Success criteria had been modified twice to fit actual results.

Test 4: Risk Tolerance (5 points - WEAK)

The organization had limited failure tolerance. The initiative was expected to succeed immediately. No contingency plans existed. Risk management was minimal.

Test 5: Evolution Capability (3 points - VERY WEAK)

Post-launch evolution rested entirely with the vendor. The organization had no internal capability to improve or adapt. The system would remain static unless the vendor updated it.

Total Score: 26 points (LIABILITY TRAJECTORY)

Pattern Recognition

The pattern was clear: strong business problem, weak organizational execution. This was vendor dependency disguised as capability building.

Leadership Decision

The CIO faced three options:

1. **Continue as-is**: Accept this as vendor service, not asset. Renegotiate contract as service agreement, not transformation project.

2. **Redesign**: Pause, rebuild internal capability first, then re-engage vendor as accelerator not solution.

3. **Terminate**: Kill the initiative, redirect $8 million to building internal scheduling expertise.

The organization chose redesign.

What Changed

1. Strategic Clarity: Revised to 11 points

Before redesign, success meant "vendor system installed." After: "30% efficiency improvement through organizational process change, with the internal team owning the AI component."

2. Capability Readiness: Improved to 10 points

The organization hired an internal AI leader and dedicated 60% of the budget to building internal capability rather than vendor services. The vendor relationship shifted from replacing internal capability to supporting internal team learning.

3. Execution Discipline: Improved to 9 points

The CIO appointed the new AI leader with empowered decision authority. Success criteria were locked. Scope discipline was enforced. Kill authority was explicitly granted.

4. Risk Tolerance: Improved to 8 points

The organization acknowledged this was high-risk. They created a contingency budget for course correction. Failure was framed as a learning investment, not a catastrophe. They scheduled a ninety-day reassessment with explicit go/no-go criteria.

5. Evolution Capability: Improved to 12 points

Post-launch, the internal team—not the vendor—would own evolution. Continuous improvement was planned and budgeted. Learning would be captured and reused.

Reassessment Results

90 days after redesign: 47 points (MODERATE ASSET POTENTIAL)

Gaps remained (Test 3 governance still weak), but trajectory had changed. The initiative now built organizational capability rather than vendor dependency.

12 months later: 55 points (STRONG MODERATE ASSET)

The organization had closed gaps. Internal capability was maturing. The vendor relationship had evolved into a genuine partnership for acceleration, not replacement.

24 months later: 61 points (STRONG ASSET)

By this point, the organization operated independently of the vendor for core capability. The system improved annually. The asset was compounding.

Key Lessons

1. **Assessment reveals truth early.** The original score of 26 would have prevented $8 million mistake if applied at start.

2. **Pattern recognition drives decisions.** The leadership team recognized "strong business case plus weak organizational execution equals vendor dependency" and chose redesign over compromise.

3. **Scores improve through deliberate action.** The 35-point improvement over twenty-four months wasn't luck—it came from systematic fixes to each weak dimension.

4. **Assets compound over time.** By year three, the initiative generated value beyond initial ROI projections. Vendor services would never have achieved that trajectory.

Getting Started: Your Next Steps

You now have the assessment methodology. Here's how to deploy it:

Week 1: Assess Current Initiatives

Choose three to five current AI initiatives. Have the core team complete the assessment for each. Don't overthink the questions—first impressions often reveal truth faster than extended analysis.

Week 2: Portfolio Analysis

Sum scores across initiatives. What's your portfolio distribution? What percentage in strong asset range? What percentage in liability range?

Week 3: Pattern Recognition

Look for patterns:

- Which tests consistently score high? Where is organizational strength?
- Which tests consistently score low? Where is organizational weakness?
- Which initiatives have the widest variance across tests? These are opportunities for targeted improvement.

Week 4: Decision Framework

For each initiative:

- Above 58: Protect and replicate this approach
- 43–57: Fix specific gaps before scaling
- 28–42: Decide whether vendor service model is appropriate
- Below 28: Kill or completely redesign

Month 2: Organizational Learning

The assessment delivers its greatest value when it becomes embedded in how you evaluate initiatives. Build it into project governance:

- Assess new initiatives before launch approval
- Reassess quarterly to track improvement

- Build initiative templates for high-scoring approaches

- Create continuous improvement processes for low-scoring dimensions

Ongoing: Portfolio Health

Track your portfolio's asset-to-liability ratio quarterly. Healthy organizations improve this ratio over time.

The healthcare organization's journey from 26 points to 61 didn't happen through wishful thinking. It happened through systematic diagnosis followed by disciplined action. Assessment reveals where you stand—but standing still isn't the point. Chapter 12 shows you what to do about it: a 30-60-90 day transformation framework that converts the patterns this assessment reveals into the operational changes that separate organizations building assets from those accumulating liabilities.

THE BOTTOM LINE

What Matters:
Organizations in the 5% assess rigorously. Organizations in the 95% hope things work out. The assessment methodology separates them. Asset-building initiatives have strong scores across all five dimensions, while liabilities cluster in capability, evolution, or execution dimensions. Single-test weakness signals specific problems: weak strategy (Test 1), vendor dependency (Test 2), governance failure (Test 3), risk mismanagement (Test 4), or decay risk (Test 5).

Track This:
- Current portfolio asset-to-liability ratio

- Percentage of initiatives in 58+ strong asset range

- Percentage of initiatives below 28 liability range

- Score trajectory over time (improving or declining?)

- Which tests score highest in your organization? Lowest?

Do This:
- Assess your three largest current AI initiatives this week using the five tests

- Calculate total score and identify weak dimensions for each

- Decide: Does this initiative deserve continued investment, require redesign, or warrant termination?

- Build assessment into governance for all future initiatives

- Track portfolio health quarterly and adjust investment accordingly

Chapter Twelve

From Assessment to Action—The 30-60-90 Day Transformation Framework

Knowing what's wrong with your AI portfolio is valuable. Knowing what to do about it is transformative. This chapter bridges assessment and action, providing a strategic framework for the first ninety days of AI transformation—whether you're inheriting a troubled program, course-correcting an existing initiative, or launching from scratch.

The hardest part of fixing an underperforming AI program isn't diagnosing the problem—it's knowing where to start when everything needs attention. After completing your asset-liability assessment, you're staring at a portfolio of liabilities requiring remediation, neutral initiatives that could become assets with the right investment, and a handful of genuine assets that deserve protection and replication. The spreadsheet tells you what's wrong. But how do you transform it?

Across AI transformation initiatives documented in aerospace, technology, and energy sectors, the pattern holds:

organizations that succeed in the first ninety days follow a disciplined approach focused on foundation-building, not firefighting. Organizations that fail jump straight to action without understanding context, or spend months analyzing without moving.

The difference between these outcomes isn't luck or resources—it's methodology. This chapter provides that methodology: a strategic framework for the first three months that creates momentum while building the foundation for sustainable transformation.

The Philosophy Behind Disciplined Transformation

Before the timelines and milestones, understand the principles that make transformation work. These aren't platitudes—they're hard-won lessons from programs that succeeded and failed.

Discovery Before Action

The instinct when inheriting a struggling AI program is to demonstrate value quickly by launching new initiatives. Resist it completely.

Organizations don't fail at AI because they're not doing enough—they fail because what they're doing isn't working. Starting another initiative before understanding why previous ones failed adds another liability to the portfolio.

Spend your first thirty days understanding the current state before changing anything. You'll discover issues invisible from the outside, identify hidden assets worth preserving, and avoid creating new problems while trying to fix old ones.

In a composite drawn from several transformation programs, a manufacturing CIO inherited an AI program with seven active pilots and pressure from the CEO to show immediate results. His instinct was to launch an eighth pilot in a high-visibility area to demonstrate momentum. Instead, he spent four weeks interviewing stakeholders and analyzing the existing portfolio.

What he discovered changed everything: five of the seven pilots had been abandoned, consuming budget but generating no value. The two pilots that showed promise were starving for resources because funding was distributed equally across all initiatives. By reallocating resources from the zombies to the viable pilots, he doubled their progress within sixty days—without launching anything new.

That's the power of discovery first. You can't fix what you don't understand.

Foundation Before Scale

The Seven Pillars build on each other. Strategic clarity enables leadership alignment. Leadership alignment enables capability building. Capability building enables effective pilots. Improving pilot discipline without first addressing strategic clarity creates better-executed projects that miss business needs.

Focus your first ninety days on foundational issues—strategy, alignment, and governance. The operational improvements in piloting, scaling, and risk management come later, after the foundation is solid.

This sequencing feels slow under pressure to deliver results. But the alternative—trying to fix everything simultaneously—overwhelms the organization and dilutes focus. Transformation leaders who attempt comprehensive change across all Seven

Pillars at once fail. Without exception. The organization couldn't absorb that much change, executive support fragmented across too many initiatives, and nothing moved far enough to show real progress.

Foundation first isn't about being cautious. It's about being effective.

Credibility Through Quick Wins

While foundation-building is essential, you also need to demonstrate value quickly. Executives who inherit troubled AI programs have limited political capital. You need to show progress before patience runs out.

The solution isn't abandoning disciplined transformation—it's incorporating deliberate quick wins that build credibility while supporting long-term objectives. These aren't cosmetic changes or pilot purgatory. They're meaningful improvements that demonstrate competence and create momentum.

Quick wins in AI transformation look like:

- Killing obvious failing pilots and reallocating resources
- Fixing glaring governance gaps that everyone knows are broken
- Accelerating a stalled pilot that's 80% done but stuck in bureaucracy
- Improving transparency with a simple portfolio dashboard

These improvements are valuable on their own and signal that change is real, not another restructuring announcement.

Coalition Before Mandate

Sustainable AI transformation requires cross-functional support. You can't mandate your way to success—you need genuine buy-in from finance, operations, risk management, and business units.

Use the first ninety days to build a coalition of supporters who understand the vision and are committed to the journey. This coalition becomes your most valuable asset when resistance emerges or competing priorities threaten momentum.

Coalition-building isn't consensus—it's ensuring the right stakeholders understand the problem deeply enough to support difficult decisions. When you need to kill a favorite project or redirect significant budget, that pre-built coalition makes the difference between "let's discuss alternatives" and "absolutely not."

In a pattern observed across several organizations, an energy sector CTO learned this lesson painfully. He developed an excellent AI strategy with clear prioritization and brutal honesty about what needed to stop. But he hadn't built his coalition first. When he presented the strategy, stakeholders whose projects were deprioritized fought back effectively. The strategy died in committee—not because it was wrong, but because he'd tried to mandate change without building support.

Six months later, he tried again—this time spending two months building his coalition before presenting any recommendations. Same strategy, completely different reception. The coalition members had already addressed concerns, traded priorities, and built shared commitment. The strategy passed unanimously.

Transparency About Reality

Don't sugarcoat problems or oversell solutions. Executives and boards respect leaders who acknowledge hard truths and propose realistic paths forward.

Your goal in the first ninety days isn't convincing leadership that everything is fine—it's demonstrating that you understand the challenges deeply and have a credible plan to address them. Transparency builds trust. Spin destroys it.

Consider a Fortune 500 organization (a composite reflecting patterns across several large enterprises) that conducted its first honest AI portfolio assessment. The results were brutal: twenty-three active initiatives, $12 million in annual spending, zero systems in production. The temptation was to soften the message —"we have some opportunities for improvement" or "several initiatives show promise."

Instead, the new CIO told the executive team the truth: they were accumulating liabilities, not building assets. Two-thirds of their initiatives would never reach production. Their vendors knew more about their AI capabilities than their internal teams did. They were on track to spend another $12 million the following year with similar results.

The CFO's response was telling: "Finally, someone who'll tell us the truth. What's your plan?"

That transparency became the foundation for everything that followed. When the CIO later recommended killing nineteen of twenty-three pilots, executives supported it because the situation had never been oversold. When transformation took longer than hoped, they stayed patient because expectations had been set realistically.

Transparency isn't pessimism—it's professional integrity.

The 30-60-90 Day Framework

With these principles established, here's how disciplined transformation unfolds across three phases. This framework maps to the Seven Pillars, strengthening them systematically rather than trying to fix everything at once.

Month 1: Discover and Assess (Days 1–30)

Month One focuses on Strategic Clarity and Leadership Alignment—the two foundational pillars. You're not making major decisions yet. You're gathering information and building understanding.

Your primary objectives are straightforward: understand how the current portfolio is organized, understand stakeholder perspectives, conduct an asset-liability assessment of existing initiatives, and synthesize findings into a clear narrative of current state. By day thirty, you should be able to tell a coherent story about where the organization stands and why.

Concretely, this means twenty hours of stakeholder interviews (executives, business unit leaders, technical teams, risk and compliance). It means a comprehensive inventory of all AI investments with an objective assessment of each. It means completing your Five-Test Assessment from Chapter 11 across all initiatives. It means documenting what's working, what's failing, and why.

This month also means identifying your coalition—who genuinely understands the problems and could become allies when difficult decisions arrive. Don't look for universal agreement. Look for people who respect truth-telling and support disciplined approaches.

Quick wins in Month One: fix a governance process that's obviously broken, improve portfolio visibility with a simple dashboard, or reallocate resources from an abandoned pilot to one showing genuine progress. Nothing dramatic. Just signals that things are changing.

Month 2: Build Foundation (Days 31–60)

Month Two builds on assessment and focuses on Capability Building and Pilot Discipline. Now you're taking action based on discovery.

Use these thirty days to establish governance structures that reflect reality. Create executive steering committees with real decision authority, not ceremonial oversight. Establish prioritization processes that distinguish between roadmap initiatives and true experiments. Build transparency mechanisms so stakeholders see portfolio status weekly, not in quarterly reviews.

More importantly, this month focuses on building the capability foundations that enable scaling later. Assess your internal data science and ML talent, identify critical capability gaps, and begin addressing them through hiring, training, or partnerships. Establish clear standards for how pilots will run, what constitutes success, and when you will decide to kill, pivot, or scale.

Consider Maria (a composite based on several technology leaders in similar situations), a CTO at a healthcare organization. She inherited a portfolio of twelve AI pilots, no governance structure, and executive frustration with slow progress. Her Month One assessment revealed that three pilots showed genuine promise but were starving for resources. Seven had been abandoned but remained on the budget. Two were repackaged vendor solutions with no real AI complexity.

In Month Two, Maria established clear governance: a weekly steering committee with the CFO, COO, and CIO; a prioritization framework that forced trade-offs; and a weekly portfolio dashboard. She reallocated $400,000 annually from the abandoned pilots to accelerate the three viable initiatives. She set up a "pilot completion task force" focused on finishing two of the three viable pilots within ninety days, not launching new ones. She didn't announce major strategic changes. She implemented better governance, made clearer prioritization decisions, and showed the organization what discipline looks like.

By day sixty, those three pilots showed measurable progress. More importantly, team members saw that leadership meant what it said about focus and execution. Defensive behavior decreased. Collaboration increased. Political opposition to difficult decisions didn't evaporate, but it shifted from ego protection to rational trade-off discussions.

Quick wins in Month Two: bring a stalled pilot to completion, reduce approval cycle time from eight weeks to two, establish daily standups for active initiatives. Nothing revolutionary. Just the operational discipline that high-performing organizations maintain routinely.

Month 3: Create Scale Readiness (Days 61–90)

Month Three focuses on Scale Strategy, Risk Management, and Continuous Evolution—the operational pillars that enable sustainable transformation beyond the initial ninety days.

By now, you've developed a clear understanding of portfolio status, established governance that reflects reality, and built the foundation for effective execution. Month Three uses this foundation to prepare for scaling. Complete your first pilots to production if possible (or demonstrate a clear path to production). Identify which pilots should scale, which should pivot, and which should stop. Establish risk management frameworks that allow safe scaling without months of approvals.

Operationally, Month Three includes: documenting lessons from Month One and Two pilots; recruiting or developing scaling teams; standing up infrastructure (data pipelines, MLOps (machine learning operations) platforms, change management processes) that enables scaling; and communicating to the board and executive team what's working, what you've learned, and what comes next.

Critical in Month Three: establish clear decision criteria for what "success" looks like in each initiative. Not vague definitions like "delivers value." Specific metrics: revenue impact, cost reduction, cycle time improvement, risk mitigation, or competitive capability. Clear enough that a first-time observer could score each initiative.

Quick wins in Month Three: launch an initial production deployment (even at small scale), establish a repeatable process for evaluating new AI opportunities, or achieve measurable business impact from Month One pilots. These create momentum heading into months four to twelve.

Adapting to Your Organizational Context

The 30-60-90 framework provides structure, but effective transformation requires adapting to your specific context. Eight common variations:

If you're in a regulated industry (healthcare, financial services, insurance): Months One and Two expand slightly as you involve compliance and risk teams in governance development. This isn't wasted time. It's front-loading work that would happen anyway. Include regulators in coalition-building early. They're not your enemies—they have legitimate risk concerns you should address.

If your organization has zero AI investment: Month One focuses on rapid capability assessment—what can you build internally, what needs external help, what's a realistic timeline? Month Two focuses on identifying your first pilot (singular, not plural) and establishing governance around it before launch, not after six pilots are already running.

If legacy business units are heavily resourced and AI is marginalized: Understand that dynamic before attempting transformation. Coalition-building becomes critical. You need business unit leaders to see AI as enabling their success, not threatening it. Quick wins must demonstrate value within business unit problems, not in abstract AI capability.

If the organization already spent heavily on AI without results: This creates psychological and political challenges. Some will defend past investments, some will demand immediate cuts, some will distrust anything new. Month One becomes even more critical—transparency about what went wrong helps the organization grieve failed investments rather than defend them.

Coalition-building focuses on moving people from "why did we waste money" to "what have we learned and what's next."

If you're in a highly distributed organization: Month One governance development takes longer because you need alignment across geographies or business units. Quick wins should demonstrate value locally first (a regional business unit's AI success), then spread that pattern.

If you're in a startup or high-growth company: The framework still applies but the timescale compresses. Assessment is faster because there are fewer initiatives. Foundation-building focuses on establishing governance before bad patterns solidify, not fixing existing dysfunction.

If board or investor pressure is extreme: Transparency becomes your strongest asset. Board members respect leaders who understand challenges deeply and have credible plans. They panic when given spin. Acknowledge the pressure, but stay disciplined. Build quick wins that matter, not cosmetic changes that create false confidence.

If you have limited budget or team: Ruthless prioritization becomes critical. You can't transform everything. You can establish governance that forces trade-offs, complete a small pilot that proves capability, and build the foundation for scaling when resources improve. Don't promise more than you can deliver.

But even the best ninety-day plan fails without honest measurement. The most dangerous AI programs aren't the ones that fail visibly—they're the ones that appear to succeed while building nothing lasting. Chapter 13 addresses the measurement

discipline that keeps transformation honest and investments
accountable.

THE BOTTOM LINE

What Matters:
The difference between transformation success and failure is determined in the first ninety days—not through heroic effort but through disciplined methodology.

Track This:
- Month 1: Portfolio assessment complete with clear narrative of current state

- Month 2: Governance structure established and quick wins delivered (measurable progress on two to three initiatives)

- Month 3: First pilots approaching production and decision criteria clear (go/no-go decision framework documented)

Do This:
1. Protect Month One discovery work despite pressure to show immediate action

2. Build coalition deliberately—identify allies before presenting major decisions

3. Deliver quick wins that support long-term strategy, not cosmetic changes

4. Establish governance that enforces prioritization before launching new initiatives

5. Maintain transparency about challenges and realistic timelines with leadership

6. Map each month to specific Seven Pillars (Month 1: Pillars 1–2, Month 2: Pillars 3–4, Month 3: Pillars 5–7)

Chapter Thirteen

Measuring What Matters—The Three-Layer Metrics Framework for AI Portfolio Health

"If you can't measure it, you can't manage it." This familiar maxim is often attributed to Peter Drucker, but he never wrote it. W. Edwards Deming came closer—and argued the opposite: "It is wrong to suppose that if you can't measure it, you can't manage it—a costly myth." The irony is instructive. In AI transformation, obsession with measurement can be as dangerous as its absence—because measuring the wrong things is worse than measuring nothing at all.

Organizations obsess over AI metrics that look impressive in board presentations while missing the fundamentals that predict success. They track models deployed, accuracy scores, and processing speed while ignoring whether anyone uses the systems, whether decisions are improving, or whether the organization is becoming more capable.

This chapter is about measuring what matters—the indicators that separate AI programs building sustainable capability from those burning money on sophisticated technology nobody uses.

The Measurement Trap

Most AI measurement frameworks fail because they optimize for what's easy to measure rather than what's meaningful to measure. This creates three common traps.

Trap 1: Vanity Metrics

These are measurements that sound impressive but don't correlate with actual value. Number of AI models deployed. Total data processed. Algorithm accuracy scores. Number of pilots launched. Percentage of employees with AI access.

These metrics indicate activity, not value. Organizations with dozens of deployed AI models generate zero business impact, while organizations with three well-designed AI systems transform operations. This pattern recurs across industries. At one Fortune 500 financial services company, leadership proudly announced they'd deployed forty-seven AI models in eighteen months. When an independent audit examined actual usage, thirty-one models had fewer than ten active users. Twelve had zero users. Four were processing data but nobody acted on the outputs. Only seven were changing decisions and creating value.

The vanity metrics looked fantastic. The business impact was negligible.

Trap 2: Lagging Indicators Without Leading Indicators

Lagging indicators tell you what happened—revenue impact, cost savings, productivity gains. Essential but insufficient, because they reveal whether you're on track only after it's too late to course-correct.

Leading indicators predict future performance. They warn you of problems before they impact results and confirm you're building capability that will generate returns over time.

One organization measured only financial returns from AI initiatives. By the time they realized an initiative failed to deliver forecasted value—often six to twelve months post-deployment—they'd already committed resources to scaling it and launched three similar initiatives. Leading indicators would have flagged adoption problems within weeks of launch, when corrections were still inexpensive.

Measuring only lagging indicators is driving by rearview mirror. You see where you've been but can't anticipate what's ahead.

Trap 3: Technology Metrics Without Business Metrics

Many organizations measure AI system performance extensively—latency, throughput, error rates, model accuracy—while barely measuring business impact. They can tell you their recommendation engine has 94.3% accuracy but not whether it's increasing revenue.

Technical metrics matter only in service of business outcomes. A perfectly accurate model that nobody uses generates zero value. A moderately accurate model that changes decisions and improves outcomes is transformative.

The Three-Layer Framework

Effective AI measurement requires three layers working together: strategic metrics that track overall program health, pillar metrics that assess maturity across foundational capabilities, and initiative metrics that evaluate individual investments.

Think of it as measuring health at three altitudes. Strategic metrics are the satellite view—is the overall program building assets or accumulating liabilities? Pillar metrics are the topographic map—which foundational capabilities are strong, which need attention? Initiative metrics are ground-level observations—is this specific AI investment delivering value?

Each layer serves different decisions. Strategic metrics inform portfolio-level resource allocation. Pillar metrics identify where to invest in capability building. Initiative metrics determine whether to kill, continue, or scale individual AI investments.

All three layers matter. Organizations that measure only at one level make poor decisions. Those measuring only strategic metrics can't diagnose what's broken. Those measuring only initiatives can't see portfolio-wide patterns. Those measuring only pillars can't connect capability to business value.

Strategic Portfolio Metrics: The Five That Matter

These metrics assess your overall AI program health. From the hundreds of potential metrics in the literature, five predict success. Detailed definitions and calculation methods are in the digital resources, but here's what matters for strategic decision-making.

Metric 1: Portfolio Asset Score

This metric applies the Asset-Liability Framework to your entire AI portfolio. What percentage of your investments are building lasting organizational capability (assets) versus creating technical debt and dependencies (liabilities)?

Calculate by scoring each initiative using the five tests from Chapter 11, then aggregating across your portfolio. Track the percentage scoring as assets versus liabilities, and most importantly, the net portfolio score.

Target trajectory: Most organizations start with 20 to 30% assets and 40 to 50% liabilities (net score of -20%). Within twelve months, aim for 60 to 70% assets and 15 to 25% liabilities (net score of +35 to 45%). By twenty-four months, target 75 to 85% assets with 10 to 15% liabilities (net score of +60 to 70%).

This is your north star metric. Everything else serves it—are you systematically building organizational capability or accumulating technical debt? When this number moves in the wrong direction, something fundamental is broken.

Metric 2: Initiative Deployment Velocity

How long does it take from initiative approval to production deployment? This metric reveals whether you're building reusable capabilities and improving processes, or rebuilding from scratch every time.

Track the average time across successful initiatives only—including failures would reward killing pilots quickly for the wrong reasons. The trend matters more than the absolute number. Are you getting faster or slower?

Organizations typically start at nine to eighteen months average deployment time. By month twelve, target four to eight months (50%+ improvement). By month twenty-four, aim for two to four months (70%+ improvement). If velocity is flat or worsening despite "experience," you're not building reusable assets. You're starting from scratch each time.

Warning signs: high variance with no clear pattern, deployment time consumed primarily by approvals rather than development, or vendor dependencies causing delays. These point to systemic problems in governance, capability, or strategy.

Metric 3: Initiative Success Rate

What percentage of AI initiatives achieve their stated business objectives and progress from pilot to production? This metric shows whether you're getting better at scoping, implementing, and deploying AI.

Count successful initiatives (delivered business value and scaled to production) as percentage of completed initiatives. Exclude ongoing pilots from the denominator—you're measuring what's completed, not what's active.

Most organizations start at a 20 to 35% success rate. Target 50%+ within twelve months, and 60%+ by twenty-four months. Best-in-class organizations sustain significantly higher success rates through rigorous selection and execution discipline. If your success rate isn't improving, your selection process or execution discipline is broken—or both.

Red flag: success rate remaining flat or declining despite experience and investment. This typically indicates weak front-end discipline (bad pilots get funded), weak implementation (good pilots fail to scale), or weak post-deployment governance (technically successful pilots don't deliver intended business value).

Metric 4: Vendor Dependency Ratio

What percentage of your AI program depends on external vendor relationships versus internal organizational capability? This metric reveals whether you're building assets or renting solutions.

Calculate as the percentage of AI initiatives requiring ongoing external support divided by total initiatives. Include dependency on specific external tools, platforms, or consultants that would create problems if removed.

Most organizations start with 70 to 85% vendor dependency. Target trajectory: twelve months to 50 to 65% dependency (significant internal capability building), twenty-four months to 35 to 50% dependency (mature internal capability with selective external support).

This metric matters because vendor dependencies become liabilities during downturns. When budgets tighten, external dependencies are the first to break. Internal capability survives.

Metric 5: ROI Realization Rate

Of the financial returns your AI initiatives forecasted, what percentage materialize? This lagging indicator is essential for credibility. Organizations claiming 500% AI ROI while suffering widespread failure rates have a realization problem.

Calculate as actual financial value delivered divided by forecasted value. Include both positive returns and negative results (cost overruns). Be honest about what counts as "value"— genuine business improvement, not accounting creativity.

Most organizations start with 40 to 50% realization rates. By month twelve, target 60 to 70%. By month twenty-four, target 75%+. If realization rates are improving, you're improving forecasting accuracy and execution discipline. If they're flat or declining, your forecasts are fiction or your execution is broken.

Pillar and Initiative Metrics: Foundation for Strategic Insight

Your five strategic metrics tell you how the AI program performs overall. Pillar metrics diagnose which foundational capabilities need attention. Initiative metrics enable course correction on individual investments.

Organizations measuring only strategic metrics can't diagnose problems. Those measuring only pillar and initiative metrics can't see portfolio patterns. You need all three layers. The digital resources provide the complete framework for pillar and initiative metrics, but here's the key insight:

Pillar metrics assess maturity across the Seven Pillars—do you have clear strategy, aligned leadership, strong capability building, disciplined pilots, sound scale strategy, effective risk management, and continuous evolution? These maturity assessments tell you which pillars need focused investment.

Initiative metrics track individual project performance— business value delivered, adoption rates, technical health, timeline accuracy. These granular metrics let you course-correct struggling pilots before they consume disproportionate resources.

The discipline of three-layer measurement is this: start with strategic metrics, use pillar metrics to diagnose, and deploy

initiative metrics to execute corrections. Don't measure
everything. Measure what informs decisions.

Measurement Systems That Fail: A Case Study

Most organizations implement measurement systems that
identify problems perfectly while creating zero pressure to solve
them. Measurement becomes a scoreboard rather than a
steering mechanism.

TechManufacture Co.—a composite based on patterns
observed across multiple manufacturing organizations—
invested in an elaborate AI measurement system. They tracked
all five strategic metrics, comprehensive pillar metrics across all
Seven Pillars, and detailed initiative metrics for every project.
They built polished dashboards. They published monthly reports
to leadership. The data was perfect.

The measurement system documented TechManufacture
Co.'s AI program but didn't improve it. After eighteen months,
they had perfect data showing gradual decline. Initiative success
rate: 28%. Deployment velocity: slowing. Vendor dependency:
growing. ROI realization: 35% of forecast. The measurement
system identified problems but created no pressure to fix them.

Measurement Done Right: FinancialServices Group

FinancialServices Group—another composite drawn from
organizations that implemented measurement effectively—took
a different approach. They implemented the five strategic
portfolio metrics initially, with clear targets and monthly

leadership review. Each metric had an owner responsible for explanation and improvement.

When their Portfolio Asset Score showed 35% liabilities, they conducted root cause analysis and discovered weak Pilot Discipline. When Initiative Success Rate stalled at 38%, they examined failures systematically and tightened approval criteria. When Vendor Dependency Ratio climbed for three consecutive months, they launched targeted hiring and training programs.

The feedback loops mattered more than the metrics themselves. FinancialServices Group used measurement to drive continuous improvement. After six months, they added pillar metrics for their weakest areas. After twelve months, they had standardized initiative metrics but tracked them only for at-risk projects.

Results after eighteen months: initiative success rate improved from 31% to 61%. Average deployment time dropped from fourteen months to seven. Vendor dependency shifted from 78% external to 54%. ROI realization climbed from 42% to 74%. Portfolio Asset Score moved from -18% to +41%.

The difference wasn't measurement sophistication— FinancialServices Group's system was simpler. The difference was discipline: measuring what mattered, acting on what they measured, and letting results validate the approach.

Building Your Measurement Program

Implement measurement progressively over your first year.

Months 1–3: Establish Baseline. Implement the five strategic portfolio metrics. Document current state across all metrics. Set up basic tracking infrastructure. Establish measurement cadence (monthly strategic review). Goal: know where you're starting from.

Months 4–6: Add Pillar Metrics. Implement maturity metrics for your weakest two to three pillars. Begin tracking trends over time. Create pillar-specific improvement plans. Link metrics to pillar initiatives. Goal: understand which capabilities need attention.

Months 7–9: Refine and Standardize. Standardize initiative-level metrics for new projects. Implement feedback loops at all levels. Train teams on metric interpretation and use. Establish clear metric ownership. Goal: make measurement operationally routine.

Months 10–12: Optimize and Mature. Retire metrics that haven't driven decisions. Add metrics for emerging needs. Automate data collection where possible. Conduct first annual strategic assessment. Goal: measurement becomes self-sustaining.

The sequence matters. Starting with too many metrics creates overhead before value is proven. Starting with strategic metrics demonstrates value quickly, making it easier to add pillar and initiative metrics later.

The Measurement Mindset

Technical measurement is straightforward—define metrics, collect data, display results. The hard part is the cultural shift that measurement demands.

From Optimism to Realism. Organizations struggle with AI measurement because accurate measurement reveals uncomfortable truths. That "successful" pilot isn't being used. That flagship AI system costs more to maintain than it saves. That strategy everyone signed off on isn't driving decisions.

Leaders who embrace measurement accept that problems will surface—and welcome it. Unknown problems can't be fixed. Visible ones can. The measurement mindset treats bad news early as good news.

From Perfection to Progress. Poor metrics early in transformation are normal. Your first asset-liability assessment might show 70% liabilities. Your initial success rate might be 25%. These aren't failures—they're baselines.

What matters is trajectory. Are you getting better quarter over quarter? Is the trend line pointing in the right direction? Are you learning from each cycle? Organizations that demand immediate success kill measurement programs before they generate value.

From Blame to Learning. The worst measurement cultures use metrics as weapons—to prove someone failed, assign blame, or justify punishment. This guarantees future metrics will be manipulated or hidden.

Healthy measurement cultures use metrics as learning tools —to understand what works, identify what doesn't, and guide improvement. When pilots fail, celebrate the fast learning. When initiatives miss targets, dig into why and apply lessons forward. When metrics reveal problems, reward the transparency and focus on solutions.

From Data to Decisions. The ultimate measurement mindset treats metrics as inputs to decisions, not ends in themselves. Every metric should answer a specific question. Should we continue or kill this pilot? Should we scale or contain this deployment? Should we invest more in this capability or redirect resources? Are we building assets or accumulating liabilities? What's blocking progress and how do we remove it?

If a metric doesn't inform a real decision, stop measuring it. The goal isn't comprehensive measurement. The goal is better decisions.

THE BOTTOM LINE

What Matters:
Most AI measurement fails because organizations measure what's easy—activity, technology metrics, vanity metrics—rather than what matters: business value, organizational capability, and strategic health. Effective measurement requires three layers working together: strategic portfolio metrics for overall health, pillar maturity metrics for capability assessment, and initiative metrics for individual investment evaluation.

Track This:
Five strategic metrics tell you whether your AI portfolio is building assets or accumulating liabilities: Portfolio Asset Score (assets vs. liabilities), Deployment Velocity (speed to production), Initiative Success Rate (pilots that reach production and deliver value), Vendor Dependency Ratio (internal vs. external investment), and ROI Realization Rate (forecasted vs. actual value). Establish regular cadence, honest accounting, clear ownership, and explicit feedback loops.

Do This:
Implement the three-layer measurement framework within sixty days. Start with the five strategic metrics at the portfolio level. Embrace realism over optimism, focus on progress over perfection, and treat metrics as learning tools rather than weapons. If a metric doesn't inform a real decision, stop measuring it.

Measurement tells you where you stand. But knowing your position raises a deeper question: what kind of organization do you need to become? Chapter 14 examines the architecture of AI-ready organizations—the strategic, technical, organizational, and cultural capabilities that separate organizations building lasting competitive advantage from those perpetually chasing the next trend.

Building Your AI-Ready Organization—The Architecture of Lasting Competitive Advantage

After twenty-five years leading technology transformations, I've learned that successful AI adoption isn't primarily a technology challenge—it's an organizational capability challenge.

The organizations succeeding with AI aren't those with the biggest budgets, the most sophisticated algorithms, or partnerships with leading AI vendors. They're organizations that built foundational capabilities making AI adoption natural, sustainable, and value-generating.

Five years from now, winners won't be distinguished by their algorithms—AI technology will be a commodity. They won't be distinguished by their budgets—money amplifies what you have, good or bad. They won't be distinguished by vendor partnerships —vendors consolidate, pivot, and fail.

Winners will be distinguished by organizational capability that compounds over time and adapts to whatever comes next.

The AI-Ready Organization: Five Distinguishing Characteristics

Walk into an AI-ready organization and you sense something different immediately. Not the technology—the culture. Not the sophistication of solutions—the discipline of execution.

Strategic AI Literacy Across Leadership

In AI-ready organizations, executive leadership understands AI well enough to make informed strategic decisions without being technical experts.

They distinguish genuine AI capabilities from vendor hype. They ask penetrating questions about AI proposals. They recognize when AI is appropriate versus other approaches. They assess AI risks and opportunities intelligently. They make strategic investment decisions without outsourcing their thinking to consultants.

This doesn't mean every executive understands neural network architectures. It means they grasp AI's capabilities, limitations, and business implications well enough to lead effectively.

The contrast is stark. In AI-dependent organizations, leadership treats AI as a black box. They approve AI investments based on vendor presentations, consultant recommendations, or competitive pressure—not because they understand what they're buying or why it matters. When asked about AI strategy, they defer to the CIO. When challenged about AI investments, they cite what competitors are doing. When AI initiatives fail, they blame technology or execution without examining the strategic decisions that set up the failure.

AI literacy isn't optional for leadership anymore. You cannot lead what you don't understand.

> **RED FLAG: The Capability Facade**
> Your organization claims AI readiness but owns no independent capability:
> - AI readiness is measured by vendor relationships and pilot counts, not internal skills
> - Leadership cannot name a single AI capability the organization owns independently
> - When asked "What can you do without vendor support?" the answer is silence
> - Readiness is defined by what you've purchased rather than what you've built

Data as Strategic Asset

AI-ready organizations treat data as a strategic asset with corresponding investment, governance, and management discipline.

They've invested in data quality management processes, clear ownership and accountability, accessible infrastructure, consistent governance, privacy and security frameworks, and literacy across the organization. Most importantly, they understand that AI quality is bounded by data quality. Sophisticated algorithms cannot compensate for poor data— garbage in, garbage out applies regardless of how advanced your models are.

The contrast: Data-challenged organizations have fragmented data with information silos across departments, inconsistent definitions of key metrics, poor data quality that nobody owns, limited accessibility requiring IT intervention, and reactive governance that's policy-heavy but implementation-light. They launch AI initiatives without fixing underlying data issues, then wonder why models underperform or require extensive manual intervention.

Data isn't infrastructure. Data is strategy. Treat it accordingly.

Experimentation Culture with Discipline

AI-ready organizations embrace experimentation—but disciplined experimentation with clear hypotheses, success criteria, and kill criteria.

They've normalized rapid pilot launches with constrained scope, explicit go/no-go criteria set upfront, fast kill decisions when criteria aren't met, systematic lessons capture from both successes and failures, and knowledge sharing across the organization.

They celebrate learning from failed experiments as much as successful deployments. Pilots that prove an approach won't work are valuable—they prevent larger investments in dead-end solutions.

The contrast: Risk-averse organizations avoid experimentation, insisting on exhaustive analysis and guarantees before trying anything. They miss opportunities because they can't move until certainty exists—which never arrives with emerging technology. Undisciplined organizations experiment constantly but learn little. Pilots proliferate without clear objectives, run indefinitely without decisions, and generate no institutional knowledge. Busy, but not learning.

The right balance isn't caution or chaos. It's disciplined experimentation that learns fast and decides faster.

Internal Capability That Compounds

AI-ready organizations have built internal expertise that grows over time through strategic hiring of core AI talent, systematic training and development, knowledge capture and documentation, communities of practice, career paths for AI expertise, and retention of institutional knowledge.

They use vendors strategically for specialized capabilities while maintaining core competencies internally. Each initiative builds organizational capability rather than just delivering a solution.

The contrast: Vendor-dependent organizations outsource AI thinking to consultants and vendors. They deploy vendor platforms but can't evaluate whether those platforms are appropriate, troubleshoot when issues arise, or adapt to changing needs. When key vendors change pricing, features, or strategic direction, these organizations have no optionality. They're captured, not partnered.

Every AI initiative should answer one question: What capability does this build that persists after the project ends?

Integration into Operating Rhythm

In AI-ready organizations, AI isn't special. AI governance and management are integrated into normal business operations, not treated as exceptional cases requiring separate processes.

AI initiatives follow standard portfolio management. AI governance is embedded in existing risk and compliance frameworks. AI performance is reviewed in regular business reviews. AI capabilities are considered in strategic planning.

The contrast: Many organizations create separate "AI labs" or "innovation centers" disconnected from core operations. These generate interesting prototypes but struggle to transition to production because they're not integrated into how the business works.

Innovation that stays in the lab isn't innovation. It's expensive theater.

The Capability Architecture: Four Domains

Building an AI-ready organization requires developing capabilities across four interconnected domains. Think of these not as checkboxes to complete but as muscles to strengthen continuously.

Strategic Capabilities: Leading with Intelligence

Strategic capabilities enable effective AI decision-making at leadership levels. Without them, you're reacting to vendors and competitors rather than directing your own path.

Core competencies include: AI strategy development connecting technology possibilities to business objectives. Investment analysis evaluating AI opportunities based on business value, not technology sophistication. Governance design that enables rather than blocks AI adoption. Portfolio management balancing innovation and efficiency across multiple initiatives.

The strategic domain isn't about understanding algorithms. It's about understanding value. Where does AI create competitive advantage in your market? Which AI capabilities are strategic versus tactical? How do you prioritize when everything seems important? How do you govern fast enough to capture opportunity but carefully enough to manage risk?

These questions don't have technical answers. They have strategic answers that technical people can't answer alone.

Technical Capabilities: Building the Foundation

Technical capabilities enable you to develop, deploy, and operate AI systems effectively. Without them, you're perpetually dependent on vendors for work you should control.

Core competencies include: Data engineering ensuring quality, accessibility, and governance. Machine learning development creating models that solve real problems. MLOps automating deployment and monitoring. Integration architecture connecting AI systems to your technology stack.

The technical domain isn't about having AI PhDs on staff—though that helps. It's about having enough internal expertise to make intelligent technical decisions, evaluate vendor claims, troubleshoot issues, and adapt to changing technology. It's the difference between using technology and being used by it.

Organizational Capabilities: Building the Machine

Organizational capabilities enable you to execute AI initiatives at scale without grinding to a halt under governance overhead.

Core competencies include: Cross-functional team structure balancing business, technology, and operations representation. Change management enabling the organization to adapt as AI transforms processes. Governance frameworks that move fast and fail safely rather than paralyze through perfectionism. Talent management attracting and retaining AI expertise.

The organizational domain isn't about org charts. It's about structure that enables initiative without bureaucracy. Most organizations have the opposite problem—they optimize for control, not capability.

Cultural Capabilities: Building the Way

Cultural capabilities determine whether AI adoption becomes lasting competitive advantage or an expensive disruption.

Core competencies include: AI literacy making AI decisions normal, not exotic. Data literacy enabling decisions based on evidence rather than intuition. Experimentation culture accepting calculated risk and learning from failure. Continuous learning mindset keeping pace with rapid technology evolution.

The cultural domain may be the most important because it's hardest to change and easiest to lose. You can hire technical talent. You can't install culture overnight.

Action: Audit your AI capabilities with one question: "What can we do without any vendor?" If the answer is nothing, you have a facade, not a foundation. Start building internal capability before your next vendor contract renewal.

> **RED FLAG: The Culture Shortcut**
> Your organization tries to install AI culture through declaration rather than earned behavioral change:
> - Leadership announces the company is "now AI-first" without changing hiring, incentives, or risk tolerance
> - Slogans and reorganizations replace genuine shifts in decision-making processes

- Employees hear the mandate but see no change in what leaders reward, tolerate, or punish
- Cultural transformation is treated as a communications exercise rather than a behavioral one

Action: Stop declaring culture and start demonstrating it. Change what you hire for, what you reward, and what you tolerate. Culture is built through daily leadership behavior, not annual announcements.

The Transformation in Practice

This pattern repeats across industries: organizations that look AI-ready on paper but crumble under scrutiny because they've purchased capability rather than built it. The contrast between facade and foundation becomes clearest when you watch a real transformation unfold.

Consider a mid-sized industrial company—call them IndustraCo, a composite drawn from several organizations whose transformation journeys share these patterns—that in 2021 found itself in a familiar position. They had eight vendor-managed AI systems running across operations: predictive maintenance, demand forecasting, quality inspection, and several optimization models. Annual AI spend exceeded $6 million. On paper, they looked sophisticated. In reality, they had zero internal machine learning capability. Every model update, every retraining cycle, every performance issue required a vendor call. When their primary vendor raised prices 30%, leadership realized they had no optionality. They weren't partnered with their vendors—they were captured by them.

The transformation that followed was unglamorous and, at times, politically painful. In the first year, IndustraCo's new AI platform lead—their first internal AI hire—focused on three things: establishing data governance that had never existed, beginning structured knowledge transfer from the primary vendor, and launching an internal training program for existing engineers. Visible progress was minimal. The board grew impatient. Executives who had approved the transformation investment wanted new AI deployments, not governance frameworks and training curricula. The AI lead held the line, arguing that building on a broken foundation would only create more expensive vendor dependency.

Year two delivered the first proof point. The internal team deployed its first internally built model—a predictive quality system for a manufacturing line that had relied on vendor-managed inspection AI. It wasn't the most sophisticated model, but it was theirs. They could update it, retrain it, explain it, and improve it without a vendor call. By year's end, vendor dependency had dropped from 100% to roughly 60%, with the internal team handling routine model updates and performance monitoring across the legacy systems.

By year three, the compounding effect was unmistakable. Five AI systems were in production—three built internally, two still vendor-managed but with full internal understanding. Vendor costs had dropped 45%. New models deployed in eight weeks versus the six months vendor-dependent development required. Most telling: the internal AI team had begun proactively advising business units on AI opportunities rather than waiting for vendor sales pitches to drive the conversation. They had shifted from consumers of AI to creators of AI capability.

The transformation wasn't dramatic in any single quarter. It was relentless across twelve of them. That's what real capability building looks like—not a vendor presentation about what's possible, but the patient, disciplined work of making it yours.

The Vision of AI Maturity: The Ten-Year Horizon

Here is what AI maturity looks like in practice, because it's different from what most organizations imagine.

Year one is humbling. You're building foundation across all four capability domains—establishing governance, hiring your first internal AI talent, fixing data quality, and earning credibility through disciplined pilots rather than splashy demos.

Year three is where the architecture matures. You've developed cross-functional teams that work without constant executive intervention. Knowledge management captures lessons systematically. Your experimentation culture has shifted from "ask permission" to "follow the framework." New initiatives build on previous ones instead of starting from scratch.

Year five is where the organization feels different. AI governance is embedded in normal business operations, not treated as a special case. Internal capability handles most initiatives without vendor dependency. Data-driven decision-making is cultural norm, not aspiration. New executives join and are surprised at how normal AI has become in daily operations.

Year ten, you've built something durable. The four capability domains reinforce each other—strategic maturity enables better technical decisions, organizational muscle enables faster cultural shifts, cultural readiness attracts stronger talent. The architecture sustains itself through leadership transitions and technology shifts because it's embedded in how the organization operates, not dependent on any individual champion.

This is hard. It's supposed to be hard. If building AI-ready organizations were easy, everyone would do it, and it wouldn't create competitive advantage.

The hard parts are where you win.

Building Blocks: Prioritization and Sequencing

With four capability domains and decade-spanning horizons, where do you start?

Foundation phase (Months 1–12): Strategic capability comes first—that's your steering wheel. Establish clear AI strategy before building. Run pilots in parallel while building strategic discipline. Select foundational technical capabilities (data architecture, ML development environment, governance framework). Begin cultural transformation through education and visible leadership commitment.

Acceleration phase (Years 2–3): Once foundation is solid, accelerate capability building across all domains. Expand technical capabilities from foundational to sophisticated. Build organizational structures supporting scale. Deepen cultural change through normalized experimentation and data-driven decision-making.

Optimization phase (Years 4–5): Refine what works. Eliminate what doesn't. Double down on sources of competitive advantage. Expand to new domains and markets. Build proprietary IP that competitors can't quickly replicate.

Sustainment phase (Years 5+): Continuous evolution that keeps you ahead of technology shifts. Maintain urgency and learning culture. Periodically reinvent as the external environment changes.

The sequencing depends on your starting point. If your strategic clarity is weak, start there. If your data foundation is broken, fix it first. If your organization can't execute pilots, address that. There's no universal sequence—only assessment followed by intelligent prioritization.

> **RED FLAG: The Perpetual Foundation**
> Your organization has been building foundation for years without progressing to execution:
> - After eighteen or more months of foundation work, zero AI applications are in production
> - The organization has governance frameworks, strategy documents, and training programs but no deployments
> - Each quarter brings new foundation requirements rather than deployment milestones
> - Foundation building has become an excuse for avoiding the risk of production
>
> **Action:** Set a hard deadline: if your foundation phase exceeds eighteen months without a production deployment, something is wrong. Foundation enables execution—it does not replace it. Ship something real.

Your Next Move

Building an AI-ready organization starts with honest assessment of where you are today.

Strategic readiness: Do you have a clear AI strategy tied to business objectives? Can your executive team articulate that strategy unprompted? Do you have portfolio management discipline? Regular strategic reviews? Governance enabling fast, safe decisions?

Technical readiness: Is your data quality sufficient for AI? Do you have internal ML development capability? MLOps practices? Reusable platform components? Integration architecture supporting AI?

Organizational readiness: Do you have cross-functional AI teams that work? Change management for AI deployments? Knowledge capture and sharing? Growing internal capability? Low vendor dependency for strategic decisions?

Cultural readiness: Do you have AI literacy across management? Experimentation normalized? Data-driven decision-making standard? Innovation mindset present? Continuous learning culture?

Be honest. Optimism about current state only delays dealing with reality. The organizations succeeding with AI aren't those that started in the best position—they're those that honestly assessed where they stood and systematically closed gaps.

Your second move is committing to the decade-long journey. This isn't a transformation project that ends. It's a permanent shift in organizational capability. Sustain investment even when returns aren't immediately visible. Build foundation even when stakeholders want impressive deployments. Maintain discipline even when pressure mounts to move faster or skip steps.

The third move is beginning. Not with grand announcements or comprehensive plans—with focused action on highest-priority gaps. Executive education if leadership lacks AI literacy. Data foundation if data quality is poor. Governance design if approval processes block progress. Internal capability building if vendor dependency is high.

Start where you are. Begin with what matters most. Build systematically. Measure progress. Adjust based on learning. Stay focused on fundamentals, especially when hype is deafening.

Five years from now, you'll either have built organizational capability that creates sustainable competitive advantage, or you'll still be chasing the next technology trend, perpetually starting over, never building anything that lasts.

The choice is yours. The time to start is now.

The detailed frameworks, assessment tools, and implementation guidance for this journey are in the companion digital resources. Use them. They represent decades of lessons learned the hard way so you don't have to.

But frameworks and tools don't build AI-ready organizations. Leaders do—leaders with the discipline to focus on fundamentals when everyone else chases sophistication, and the patience to build capability when stakeholders demand immediate results.

THE BOTTOM LINE

What Matters:
Building an AI-ready organization requires developing four
interconnected capability domains—strategic, technical,
organizational, and cultural—that compound over time. Five
characteristics distinguish AI-ready organizations from the
rest: they treat AI as a leadership discipline, build internal
capability before scaling vendor partnerships, prioritize
organizational learning over individual expertise, design for
evolution rather than perfection, and measure capability
growth alongside business value.

Track This:
Maturity levels across all four capability domains. Track the
ratio of internal capability to vendor dependency. Monitor
whether each AI initiative strengthens organizational muscle
or merely rents external functionality. Measure leadership
engagement depth, not just executive sponsorship breadth.

Do This:
Assess your organization honestly against the four capability
domains within thirty days. Identify the domain where you
are weakest—that is your highest-leverage starting point.
Within sixty days, launch a focused initiative to build
foundational capability in that domain. Sequence your
investments: don't try to build everything simultaneously.
Prioritize the capabilities that enable all others.

The organizational architecture described in this chapter is
not something you install in a quarter. It requires sustained
investment across all four capability domains. The next
chapter examines the economics of that sustained investment

—why organizations that play the long game build advantages that short-term optimizers cannot match.

<hr>

PART IV: THE PATH FORWARD

Chapter Fifteen

The Long Game

Beyond the Transformation

Most AI strategies optimize for quarters. The rare few that build lasting capability optimize for decades.

Consider two composite organizations representing patterns observed across dozens of AI programs. Both invested $50 million in AI capabilities. Organization A deployed dozens of AI pilots on vendor platforms, celebrated rapid deployment, and showcased impressive demonstrations at board meetings. Organization B built internal ML infrastructure, developed data platforms, trained engineers, established governance, and ran far fewer visible pilots.

By 2018, Organization A had eighty AI pilots running. Organization B had fifteen production systems. The board loved Organization A's innovation dashboard. Nobody questioned their approach.

By 2020, everything changed. Organization A's pilots hadn't scaled. Vendor relationships had become dependencies. Cost per initiative wasn't decreasing—it was increasing. Internal capability hadn't grown. When COVID forced budget scrutiny, they couldn't defend their investments. They killed sixty pilots and struggled to maintain the remaining twenty.

Organization B was accelerating. Their fifteenth AI system cost 40% less to build than their first. Internal capability enabled rapid response to pandemic disruptions. They built and deployed six COVID-response systems in eight weeks. Platform investments from 2015–2018 were generating compound returns.

By 2025, the gap was decisive. Organization A was still sorting out fundamentals, dependent on vendors, repeating mistakes. Organization B had become AI-native—machine learning was just "how we work," capability was an asymmetric advantage, and strategic flexibility was expanding rather than narrowing.

Same starting point. Same initial investment. Radically different trajectories. The difference wasn't intelligence—both had smart teams. It wasn't budget—both spent similar amounts. It wasn't technology—both had access to the same tools.

The difference was time horizon. Organization A optimized for quarterly results and board presentations. Organization B optimized for compound capability growth over decades.

This is the essence of the long game: the economics of sustained investment create advantages that short-term optimization cannot match. While most organizations chase quarterly results, the disciplined minority build platforms whose returns compound with every passing year.

The long game isn't about predicting which AI technology wins. It's about investing with a time horizon that transforms costs into assets. Chapter 14 described the organizational architecture required. This chapter examines why that architecture, sustained over years, creates economic advantages that grow rather than erode—and how to protect those investments when short-term pressure mounts.

The Sustained Advantage Framework

Long-term AI advantage doesn't come from deploying more systems or adopting newer technologies faster. It comes from organizational capability that persists, compounds, and adapts faster than the market shifts.

Building Enduring Capabilities

The organizations that dominate in 2035 won't be those who deployed the most AI systems in 2025. They'll be organizations that built capabilities enabling continuous AI innovation at decreasing marginal cost with expanding strategic flexibility.

Enduring capabilities have four characteristics:

Platform Economics: Initial investments enable subsequent initiatives at dramatically lower marginal cost. AI-mature organizations achieve 60% or greater cost reductions per initiative by their twentieth system compared to their first. This isn't vendor discounts—it's reusable components, institutional knowledge, streamlined processes, and compound expertise.

Platform-powered organizations build data infrastructure once and use it across hundreds of applications. They develop MLOps capabilities that enable model deployment in weeks, not months. They create governance frameworks that enable fast, confident decisions. Their tenth AI system doesn't require rebuilding foundation—it draws on accumulated capability.

Organizations lacking platform thinking treat each AI initiative as standalone. Every system requires custom data pipelines, unique infrastructure, new vendor relationships, separate governance approvals. Their twentieth initiative costs as much as their first because they're not learning systematically. They start over every time.

Capability Transfer: Expertise developed in one domain transfers to adjacent domains with minimal investment. Organizations with deep internal ML capability move from predictive maintenance to customer churn prevention to fraud detection without starting from scratch. The technical skills, processes, and organizational muscles carry over.

Organizations dependent on external capability face far higher switching costs. Moving from marketing analytics to supply chain optimization means finding new consultants, negotiating new contracts, relearning processes. Each domain shift means starting over because capability was never internalized.

Organizations with strong internal capability enter new AI domains significantly faster than those dependent on external expertise. The gap compounds: organizations with transfer capacity explore more opportunities while constrained organizations move linearly.

Strategic Independence: Capability provides options. Organizations evaluate vendor proposals objectively, bring critical capabilities in-house when needed, switch vendors without business disruption, and negotiate from strength. Strategic independence doesn't mean avoiding vendors—it means maintaining the ability to choose freely.

Organizations lacking independence face constraints that narrow over time. Vendor dependencies limit strategic options. Platform lock-in prevents optimization. Expertise concentrated in consultants walks out when contracts end. Each decision reduces future flexibility until the organization finds itself executing someone else's roadmap rather than its own strategy.

Adaptation Speed: The most valuable capability is building new capabilities faster than the market changes. Organizations that master learning compress the time from "we need this" to "we have this" from years to months. As AI technology evolves, adaptation speed determines who capitalizes on new possibilities and who watches competitors pull ahead.

Learning-centric organizations compress capability acquisition from years to months. Over a decade, this compounds into a decisive advantage. The organization that masters learning develops new capabilities at multiples of the speed of organizations still purchasing capability externally.

Portfolio Management for Compound Advantage

Individual AI systems matter less than portfolio dynamics. Organizations win the long game through portfolio management that compounds returns.

Portfolio economics should improve over time through:

Decreasing marginal costs: Your twentieth AI initiative should cost significantly less than your first. If it doesn't, you're not building capability—you're purchasing it repeatedly. Track cost per initiative over time. If the trend isn't downward, your portfolio lacks platform effects and institutional learning.

Organizations building enduring capability see consistent cost improvements—significant reductions between early initiatives, accelerating gains as platform effects and institutional learning compound, then tapering improvements beyond the twentieth. This comes from reusable infrastructure, accumulated expertise, streamlined processes, and reduced vendor dependency.

Accelerating deployment velocity: Your tenth system should reach production faster than your first. Mature organizations compress concept-to-production time from twelve or more months to eight to twelve weeks through accumulated capability, proven processes, established governance, and automated infrastructure.

Expanding capability breadth: Your portfolio should address increasingly diverse business problems without proportional resource increases. Platform investments enable exploration of new domains. Institutional knowledge transfers across contexts. Governance that enabled healthcare AI applications adapts to financial services with minor modifications.

Organizations without portfolio effects find each new domain requires starting over. Healthcare AI demands different consultants than supply chain AI. Marketing analytics demands different platforms than operations analytics. Nothing transfers, accumulates, or compounds.

Strengthening strategic position: Each initiative should increase your options for the next one. Building ML infrastructure enables capabilities that were previously impossible. Developing internal expertise reduces vendor dependence. Establishing governance enables confident risk-taking. Every investment should expand strategic degrees of freedom, not narrow them.

> **RED FLAG: Quarterly Optimization**
> Your organization sacrifices long-term capability for short-term budget targets:
> - Platform and capability investments are the first cuts during budget pressure
> - Each round of underinvestment raises cost-per-initiative, increasing future budget pressure
> - Leadership defends cuts as "pragmatic" without calculating compounding capability loss
> - Competitors who maintain capability investment during downturns pull ahead permanently
>
> **Action:** Defend capability investments during downturns—this is when long-game organizations separate from the pack. Calculate the compound cost of capability gaps, not just the quarterly savings from cuts.

Competitive Positioning Through Capability

Long-term competitive advantage comes from capability that competitors cannot quickly replicate or purchase.

Capability-based competition has three dimensions:

Speed advantages: Organizations with mature AI capability respond to market changes, competitive threats, and new opportunities faster than those dependent on external help. When COVID emerged, organizations with internal capability pivoted to pandemic response in weeks. Organizations dependent on consultants waited months for expertise availability and proposal cycles.

Cost advantages: Organizations with platform economics achieve dramatically lower costs per capability unit. Their economics enable pricing strategies, margin structures, and growth investments that vendor-dependent organizations cannot match.

Flexibility advantages: Organizations with internal capability can combine capabilities in novel ways, customize solutions to customer needs, and migrate between technological paradigms without business disruption. Capability creates optionality. Optionality creates advantage.

These advantages don't emerge overnight. They require disciplined investment in internal capability building—particularly where vendor solutions are readily available. Many leaders skip the capability investment because it's invisible while the cost is immediate. Showing board members an impressive vendor demo is easier than justifying an internal MLOps team.

But patience compounds. Organizations that maintain internal capability investment through skepticism, budget cuts, and leadership transitions emerge with decisive advantages when the market rewards capability over quick deployment.

> **RED FLAG: Capability Outsourcing**
> Your organization outsources core AI capability and calls it strategy:
> - External consultants make major AI architecture decisions
> - Vendors build proprietary systems that your team cannot maintain or evolve
> - Internal staff lack the expertise to evaluate critical technical decisions independently
> - Strategic independence is an illusion—vendor incentives drive your direction
>
> **Action:** Distinguish core from support. Core capability—architecture decisions, strategic direction, proprietary models—must be internal. Support functions can be outsourced. If your

vendor disappeared tomorrow, could you continue? If not, start building internal capability now.

The Culture of Mastery

Chapter 14 described the organizational architecture for building AI capability—the four domains, the practices, the structures. The long-game question is different: what are the economic consequences of getting that architecture right versus wrong over a decade?

The answer is a self-reinforcing cycle that either compounds advantage or compounds disadvantage. Organizations with strong internal capability attract talented engineers, which strengthens capability further, which improves competitive position, which attracts more talent. Organizations without this cycle stagnate—talented people leave for better growth, capability gaps widen, vendor dependency deepens, and costs per initiative rise rather than fall.

This cycle explains why the gap between long-game organizations and short-term optimizers widens so dramatically over time. It's not linear improvement—it's compound advantage driven by the same organizational architecture operating year after year.

> **RED FLAG: Perpetual Restart**
> Every new initiative starts from scratch with no platform effects:
> - Different tools, processes, consultants, and approaches for each project
> - By the twentieth system, cost-per-initiative hasn't decreased
> - Teams cannot articulate what they're reusing from previous work

- Infrastructure, processes, governance, and knowledge fail to transfer across initiatives

Action: After your fifth AI initiative, audit reuse. If cost-per-initiative isn't declining, your portfolio lacks platform effects. Invest in shared infrastructure, standardized processes, and knowledge capture that compounds across projects.

Long Game Mistakes

Organizations pursuing long-game advantage often fail through specific, preventable mistakes:

Mistaking activity for capability: Building fifty pilots isn't capability building if only five reach production. Deploying new technologies because they're interesting isn't capability building if they don't address strategic gaps. The long game demands intentional development focused on competitive advantage, not technology entertainment.

Confusing outsourced services with internalized capability: Contracting a vendor to build an AI system isn't capability building. It's capability purchasing. Development requires your team building systems, learning from problems, improving processes, and strengthening expertise. Outsourcing can supplement internal capability but cannot replace it.

Optimizing for short-term metrics over long-term indicators: Quarterly ROI targets undermine long-term capability building because foundational investments rarely show short-term returns. Organizations that measure success purely through immediate financial metrics consistently under-invest in capability. The long game requires patience and metrics that track capability trajectory, not just current-quarter returns.

Failing to protect platform investments from short-term pressure: During budget constraints, platform investments are easy targets because they lack direct ROI stories. Organizations that cut them during downturns regret it when conditions accelerate and they lack the foundation to respond. Protecting long-term strategic investments under short-term pressure separates winners from casualties.

Treating technology choice as capability: Adopting the latest framework, cloud platform, or AI technology isn't capability building. Capability emerges from the organization's mastery of tools, not the tools themselves. Technology changes. Capability—learning speed, pattern recognition, judgment, discipline—persists.

Long Game in Action: The Economics of Patience

Chapter 14's IndustraCo example showed what organizational transformation looks like—the governance, the knowledge transfer, the cultural shifts. This example shows what long-game economics look like when that organizational architecture operates over time.

A healthcare organization—a composite based on several health systems whose long-game economics followed similar trajectories—committed to building internal capability systematically rather than purchasing another vendor solution. The economics of their first five years tell the story:

Year one: $15 million invested in data infrastructure and first production system. No visible returns. Board-level pressure to show results.

Year two: $8 million invested. Pilot success rate improved from 8% to 35%—not from better data scientists, but from reusable processes and infrastructure.

Year three: Three production systems deployed. Cost per system: 40% lower than year one. Deployment time: 60% faster. Platform investments from years one and two were generating returns.

Year four: Five systems deployed. Thirty percent of year-four work reused previous projects. The internal team handled 80% of work previously outsourced. Vendor costs declining.

Year five: Seven systems deployed. Cost per system: $2 million—down from $15 million for the first. Same quality. Same rigor. Strategic flexibility expanding—they prioritized opportunities based on business value, not vendor availability.

The cost trajectory is the point. First system: $15 million. Twentieth system: $2 million. That 87% cost reduction didn't come from vendor discounts or cheaper technology. It came from platform economics, institutional knowledge, and streamlined processes—the compound returns of sustained capability investment that short-term optimizers never achieve.

The long game creates conditions for success. But conditions don't execute themselves. Chapter 16 addresses the final, most personal element: the leadership discipline that determines whether organizations join the disciplined minority or remain part of the majority still searching for shortcuts that don't exist.

Position for the Future

The organizations dominating in 2035 won't be those that deployed the most AI in 2025. They'll be the ones that played the long game while others chased quarterly results.

You're in position to be one of them. Long game positioning requires three commitments:

First: Recognize that quarterly results and long-term capability building sometimes conflict. When they do, protect the long-term investments. Most organizations fail the long game because they sacrifice strategic capability for short-term metrics. Winners know the difference.

Second: Measure what matters. Your portfolio should show declining cost per initiative, accelerating deployment velocity, expanding strategic independence, and increasing learning velocity. If these metrics aren't improving, you lack long-game positioning regardless of how many pilots you've deployed.

Third: Defend platform investments through market uncertainty. When markets correct, budget pressure intensifies, and AI skepticism rises, long-game organizations maintain strategic capability investments precisely because this is when they pull ahead of competitors cutting for quarterly survival.

THE BOTTOM LINE

What Matters:
Organizations don't win through deploying more pilots or adopting newer technologies faster. They win through systematic capability building that enables compound advantage across decades, not quarters.

Track This:
Cost per initiative (should decrease 20 to 30% between initiatives one through five, another 30 to 40% between five and twenty). Deployment velocity (should improve 40 to 60% over time). Strategic independence (should increase as vendor dependency decreases). Learning velocity (new team members should reach productivity faster).

Do This:
Evaluate your current strategy through long-game lens. If executed perfectly, will your capability be increasing or decreasing in five years? Will you have expanding or narrowing strategic options? Will you be building advantage or accumulating dependencies? Use this honest assessment to shift strategy if needed.

Chapter Sixteen

The Leadership Imperative —The Rare Discipline That Separates Success from Failure

I've spent twenty-five years leading technology organizations. I've seen technologies come and go, witnessed countless "transformational" trends, and watched hundreds of leaders face disruption. Through it all, one truth remains constant: technology challenges are never about technology.

They're about leadership.

AI is no different. The organizations succeeding with AI aren't those with the biggest budgets, smartest algorithms, or best vendor partnerships. They're organizations led by people who understand a fundamental truth: **AI transformation requires leadership discipline that's rare, difficult, and completely non-technical.**

This chapter is about that discipline—what it looks like, why it's hard, and how to develop it.

The Leadership Gap

The AI leadership gap isn't what most people think. It's not about technical knowledge—most technology leaders understand AI fundamentals well enough. The gap runs deeper:

Most leaders lack the discipline to focus on basics when advanced techniques are available.

It's the same pattern I've observed in martial arts for decades. Advanced practitioners get bored with fundamentals and chase exotic techniques. They know hundreds of complicated moves but can't execute a perfect basic stance under pressure.

Then they face someone who's mastered the basics. Someone whose foundation is so solid that advanced techniques build naturally upon it. Someone who's practiced basic strikes ten thousand times rather than ten thousand different strikes once.

The fundamentals practitioner wins. Every time.

AI leadership is no different. Leaders chase sophisticated AI applications—generative AI, autonomous systems, complex multi-model architectures—while neglecting basics: Strategic Clarity, Leadership Alignment, Capability Building, Pilot Discipline, Scale Strategy, Risk Management, Continuous Evolution.

The Seven Pillars aren't revolutionary. They're basic leadership principles every executive should have mastered decades ago. What makes them powerful in AI is that almost nobody executes them with discipline.

The Discipline Mindset

When I tell executives that AI success requires mastering basics, I see disappointment. Basics aren't exciting. They don't make compelling board presentations. They don't generate buzz or headlines.

This is the first test of leadership: **Are you capable of doing what works even when it's not what excites you?**

Discipline Means:

Saying No More Than Yes

Every AI opportunity looks promising in isolation. Exciting use cases. Impressive vendor demonstrations. Enthusiastic sponsors.

Disciplined leaders know that saying yes to everything means succeeding at nothing. They apply the "Five No" rule: for every AI initiative they approve, they reject five others. Not because those five are bad ideas—because focus matters more than coverage.

This requires disappointing people. Telling enthusiastic business leaders that their AI vision doesn't align with strategic priorities. Rejecting vendor proposals that solve problems you don't have. Declining board requests to "explore" technologies that distract from fundamentals.

Most leaders can't do this. The pressure to appear supportive, innovative, and responsive overpowers their commitment to strategic focus.

Killing Pilots That Aren't Working

Disciplined leaders kill failing pilots without hesitation—the zombie pilot epidemic described in Chapter 7 is one of the most common symptoms of missing discipline. They establish go/no-go criteria before pilots begin. They enforce ninety-day decision windows. They accept that sunk costs never justify continued investment.

This means admitting failure publicly. Telling executives who championed pilots that their initiatives aren't working. Accepting that experimentation sometimes reveals what doesn't work.

Most leaders dodge these conversations. They let pilots drift, hoping something changes or attention shifts elsewhere.

> **RED FLAG: The Sophistication Trap**
> Your organization pursues complex AI architectures because simplicity feels insufficient:
> - Teams evaluate multi-model ensembles, custom fine-tuning, or autonomous agent frameworks when a straightforward model would solve the problem
> - Architecture decisions are driven by how impressive the technology sounds, not what the problem requires
> - Investment size creates pressure to deploy proportionally complex solutions
> - Sophistication impresses conference audiences while simplicity delivers business value
>
> **Action:** For every AI initiative, ask: "What is the simplest approach that solves this business problem?" Start there. Escalate complexity only when simple approaches demonstrably fail.

Investing in Foundation When Pressure Demands Results

Boards want demonstrations of AI capability. Stakeholders want pilots and deployments. The pressure to "do something impressive" is relentless.

Disciplined leaders resist. They invest time understanding current state, building governance, developing capability, and establishing platforms—even when stakeholders demand visible progress.

This takes confidence—telling boards: "We're not launching new initiatives this quarter because we're building the foundation that makes future initiatives successful."

Most leaders buckle. The pressure for visible progress overpowers the commitment to foundation.

Maintaining Standards When Exceptions Seem Reasonable

Every decision to bypass governance, skip assessment, rush deployment, or bend standards seems reasonable in context. Critical business opportunity. Vendor offer expiring. Impatient executive sponsor. "This situation is different."

Disciplined leaders hold the line even when exceptions seem justified. They know that erosion happens one "reasonable exception" at a time.

Ask yourself honestly:

- Have I said no to AI initiatives that didn't meet strategic criteria even when sponsors were disappointed?

- Have I killed pilots that weren't working rather than letting them drift indefinitely?

- Have I invested in foundation when pressure demanded visible results?

- Have I maintained standards when making exceptions seemed justified?

If you answered no to any question, you're struggling with leadership discipline. This is normal—discipline is hard. But recognizing the gap is the first step toward closing it.

The Humility Requirement

The second crucial leadership quality for AI success is humility—the willingness to acknowledge what you don't know and to focus on what drives results rather than what makes you feel smart.

Humility Means: Admitting "I Don't Know"

Most executives feel pressure to have answers. Admitting uncertainty feels weak, especially with emerging technology where everyone claims expertise.

But effective AI leadership demands honest acknowledgment of uncertainty:

- "I don't know whether this AI approach will work—that's why we're piloting it"

- "I don't understand this vendor's architecture deeply enough to evaluate it—let me get technical experts involved"

- "I can't predict which AI technologies will matter five years from now—so we're building adaptable capability"

Leaders who admit uncertainty make better decisions. They seek expertise, design experiments, build flexibility, and avoid overcommitting before validation.

Leaders who pretend certainty make worse decisions. They rely on limited information, commit prematurely, double down when wrong, and optimize for appearing smart rather than being effective.

Valuing Expertise Over Status

AI decisions should reflect the judgment of people with relevant expertise, regardless of title or seniority. This sounds obvious. It rarely happens.

Humble leaders create environments where:

- Junior technical experts can challenge executive assumptions

- Data and analysis matter more than opinion and politics

- Subject matter expertise is valued regardless of rank

- Dissenting views are welcomed, not punished

- Decisions reflect best available information, not loudest voice

Learning From Failure Without Defensiveness

Failed AI initiatives reveal truths about organizational capability, market reality, and strategy effectiveness. But only if leaders examine failures without defensiveness.

Defensive leaders blame failures on execution, vendors, or bad luck. They avoid examining their own role. They discourage honest post-mortems. They change the subject when failures surface. They repeat the same mistakes.

Humble leaders own their failures. They conduct honest retrospectives. They share lessons publicly. They adjust their approach based on what they learn. They create psychological safety for others to acknowledge failures.

> **RED FLAG: The Pattern Repeater**
>
> Your organization repeats the same AI failure patterns across successive initiatives:
>
> - The third pilot has the same problems as the first—unclear success criteria, no go/no-go decisions, vendor dependency, scope creep
> - Nobody has connected the dots across failed initiatives
> - Honest retrospectives are skipped or sanitized into blameless non-findings
> - Each failure wastes not just the initiative investment but the diagnostic lesson it contained
>
> **Action:** After every AI initiative—success or failure—conduct an honest retrospective. Document patterns across initiatives, not just within them. If the same problems recur, the issue is organizational capability, not project execution.

Focusing on Effectiveness Over Sophistication

The most sophisticated AI solution isn't always the most effective. A simple rules-based system can outperform complex machine learning. Manual processes can prove more reliable than automation. Waiting for technology to mature can beat deploying immature solutions.

Humble leaders optimize for business outcomes, not technical impressiveness. They're willing to choose boring solutions that work over exciting solutions that don't.

> **RED FLAG: The Delegation Escape**
> Leadership delegates AI strategy entirely because "it's too technical for me":
> - The CIO or CTO cannot explain the AI strategy without referencing a consultant's framework or a vendor's roadmap
> - Strategic direction reflects vendor revenue targets rather than organizational priorities
> - Executives approve AI investments they cannot evaluate independently
> - "Too technical" becomes the excuse for abdicating strategic responsibility
>
> **Action:** AI strategy is leadership strategy. You can delegate execution. You cannot delegate direction. If you cannot explain your AI strategy without vendor slides, invest in your own understanding before your next board meeting.

Navigating the Politics

Leadership discipline requires handling three recurring political challenges. These aren't problems to solve once—they're ongoing tensions to manage.

Challenge 1: The Ambitious Executive

Every organization has executives with genuine enthusiasm for AI—smart, politically connected, and convinced their particular vision will transform the business.

The challenge: their vision rarely aligns with the strategic priorities you've established. Their timeline is optimistic. Their resource estimates are thin. Their political capital is substantial.

The disciplined response:

- Don't reject their vision—redirect it toward strategic priorities

- Provide genuine feedback on what would make it viable

- If it's truly misaligned, decline respectfully but clearly

- Accept their disappointment without capitulating

- Maintain relationship for future opportunities when priorities align

Challenge 2: The Board's Pressure

Boards want evidence that leadership understands AI. They want demonstrations that the organization is "doing AI." They want quarterly proof of progress.

The challenge: the work that matters—foundation building, governance creation, capability development—produces no headlines. It doesn't photograph well. It's hard to celebrate in board meetings.

The disciplined response:

- Communicate progress in ways boards understand (capability roadmaps, risk reduction, competitive positioning)

- Celebrate early wins without overstating their significance

- Educate boards on why foundation matters more than demonstrations

- Find one production pilot that validates your approach and showcase it relentlessly

- Accept that boards will never be as excited about discipline as about disruption

Challenge 3: The Team's Morale

When leaders say no to exciting initiatives, kill promising pilots, and demand rigor over speed, teams notice. Technical teams in particular want to chase cutting-edge techniques.

The challenge: morale suffers when people feel constrained rather than enabled. When discipline feels like obstruction. When foundational work feels like punishment compared to peers at companies chasing moonshots.

The disciplined response:

- Acknowledge that discipline is harder than chaos

- Celebrate discipline as competitive advantage, not limitation

- Share stories of other organizations that succeeded through discipline

- Ensure team learns continuously (discipline creates time for learning)

- Recognize and reward people who embrace fundamentals enthusiastically

The Choice

This is where the book ends and your work begins. You understand the problem. You've seen the frameworks. You know what the 5% do differently.

You face a choice.

Path 1: Join the 95%

Optimize for what excites stakeholders rather than what drives results. Chase sophisticated solutions while neglecting foundations. Pursue new technologies while avoiding difficult leadership conversations. Launch many pilots and let several drift indefinitely. Let standards erode when exceptions seem justified. Blame vendors when results disappoint.

This path is easier. It generates impressive presentations. It attracts talent who want to work with cutting-edge technology. It makes you feel like you're leading transformation.

It also leads to the 95% failure rate.

Path 2: Master the Basics

Focus on fundamentals. Build strategic clarity. Achieve cross-functional alignment. Develop internal capability. Implement pilot discipline. Scale deliberately. Manage risk proactively. Learn continuously.

This path is harder. It requires discipline when everyone else chases trends. It demands patience when stakeholders want immediate results. It takes courage to acknowledge what you don't know and learn it properly. It means disappointing people who want excitement over effectiveness.

But it leads to the 5% success rate. Organizations building sustainable competitive advantage. AI portfolios that compound as strategic assets over time. Capabilities that persist through technology cycles and leadership changes.

You'll have fewer stories about ambitious initiatives. But you'll have results. Measurable, sustainable competitive advantage.

The choice is yours.

But understand this: you cannot choose the destination without choosing the path. You cannot achieve the 5% outcomes through the 95% approach. You cannot build sustainable advantage through unsustainable practices.

The difference isn't technical knowledge. It's not budget. It's not vendor selection.

It's leadership discipline.

Discipline to focus on basics when advanced techniques are available.

Discipline to say no when yes seems easier.

Discipline to build foundation when stakeholders demand results.

Discipline to maintain standards when exceptions seem justified.

Discipline to admit uncertainty and learn rather than pretend expertise.

Discipline to measure honestly and kill what's not working.

Discipline to persist through the multi-year journey when others quit.

This discipline is rare. It's difficult. It's completely non-technical.

And it's the only thing that matters.

The Master's Journey

Let me tell you about Sarah Chen—a composite drawn from several leaders whose experiences illustrate what disciplined AI transformation looks like in practice.

When Sarah took over as CIO of a global manufacturing company in 2019, she inherited what looked like AI success: nineteen active AI pilots, partnerships with three prestigious vendors, a dedicated AI lab with PhD researchers, and board presentations showing impressive technical capabilities.

Within three months, she saw the truth. The moment it crystallized came in a scene that repeats across organizations: a quarterly review where the AI lab presented a breakthrough in predictive modeling, while an operations leader in the back row muttered, loud enough for everyone to hear, "That's great, but my line's been down twice this week and nobody can tell me why." Not one pilot had reached production. The vendors excelled at demonstrations but couldn't deliver operational systems. The AI lab published papers while the business struggled with basic process inefficiencies. The impressive technical capabilities created no business value.

She faced a choice: continue the pattern—chase more sophisticated techniques, launch more pilots, present more impressive demos—or do something harder.

She chose discipline.

She killed fifteen of the nineteen pilots—the ones "in progress" for over a year with no clear path to production, the politically connected initiatives with powerful sponsors but no business case, and the technically interesting projects that solved problems the business didn't have.

The reaction was predictable: outrage from sponsors, accusations that she "didn't understand AI," and pressure from the board to "show progress" rather than "destroy momentum."

She held firm. She spent six months on foundation—building strategic clarity, achieving genuine cross-functional alignment, developing internal capability, establishing governance that enabled rather than impeded, and creating platforms for future initiatives.

No new pilots. No vendor demos. No impressive board presentations about cutting-edge technology.

Just disciplined execution of basics.

The board grew impatient. Two executives lobbied to replace her. The pressure to demonstrate "AI leadership" was intense.

Then one of the three surviving pilots—a focused supply chain optimization application—made it to production. Not because it used the most advanced algorithms. Not because the vendor was prestigious. Because the foundation was solid: strategic clarity, cross-functional ownership, internal capability, disciplined scaling.

It generated $18 million in first-year value. Not projected value. Actual, measured, audited results.

The second pilot followed six months later. Then the third. Each built on the platform and capability developed during those six months of foundation work. Each delivered faster and at lower cost than the originals because the infrastructure existed.

Three years later, Sarah's organization ran twenty-three AI applications in production. Not pilots—production. Real business value. Sustainable operations. Internal capability that didn't depend on vendor support.

The AI lab now worked on business problems, not academic papers. The vendors were partners, not dependencies. The board presentations showed business outcomes, not technical capabilities.

Sarah's organization joined the 5%.

When asked what made the difference, the answer that emerged from leaders like Sarah captures the pattern:

"In martial arts, a black belt doesn't mean you've mastered advanced techniques. It means you've perfected the basics so thoroughly that advanced techniques become possible. AI leadership works the same way. Most executives want to skip to the advanced moves—the black belt without the years of disciplined practice. But there are no shortcuts. Master the basics or fail. It's that simple."

That insight is right.

THE BOTTOM LINE

What Matters:
The 95/5 split isn't about technology budgets, vendor selection, or technical sophistication. It's about leadership discipline— the willingness to master fundamentals when pressure mounts to chase trends, the humility to acknowledge gaps honestly, and the courage to kill initiatives that aren't working. The organizations that succeed treat AI transformation as a multi-year leadership commitment, not a technology deployment.

Track This:
Whether your organization consistently executes fundamentals across all Seven Pillars or chronically skips to advanced techniques. Monitor whether leadership engagement deepens over time or decays after initial enthusiasm. Measure the gap between what your AI program promises and what it delivers—that gap reveals your discipline deficit.

Do This:
Commit to one discipline: honest self-assessment. Score your organization against the Seven Pillars within the next week. Identify the pillar where the gap between aspiration and reality is widest. Focus there first. Build the habit of disciplined execution before expanding scope. The fundamentals practitioner always wins—not because basics are exciting, but because when pressure comes, only perfect basics survive.

Your Turn

This book has given you the framework. The Seven Pillars. The assessment tools. The implementation roadmap. The cautionary tales and success stories.

But frameworks don't matter without the discipline to execute them.

The Seven Pillars won't help if you chase sophisticated solutions while neglecting basics.

The assessment tools are worthless if you can't honestly acknowledge gaps.

The roadmap leads nowhere if you demand immediate results over sustained progress.

The question isn't whether you understand what to do. The question is whether you have the discipline to do it.

Can you focus on basics when advanced techniques are available?

Can you say no more than yes?

Can you invest in foundation when pressure demands results?

Can you maintain standards when exceptions seem reasonable?

Can you admit "I don't know"?

Can you value expertise over status?

Can you learn from failure without defensiveness?

Can you optimize for effectiveness over sophistication?

Can you persist through the multi-year journey?

These aren't technical questions. They're leadership questions. And your answers will determine whether your organization joins the 95% or the 5%.

The fundamentals practitioner always wins. In martial arts. In AI transformation. In life.

Not because fundamentals are exciting. Not because basics make great presentations. Because when pressure comes—and it always comes—only the practitioner with perfect basics survives.

Your AI future isn't determined by budget, technology, or vendors.

It's determined by leadership discipline.

The choice is yours.

Choose wisely.

Resources Guide

Your Digital Resource Library

This book provides frameworks, assessments, and implementation guidance across sixteen chapters. But mastering AI leadership requires ongoing practice with current tools and updated insights.

Readers of *Why AI Fails* receive complimentary access to a digital resource library at **www.whyaifails.com**.

What You'll Find

Assessment Tools (8 Interactive Tools)

- Strategic Clarity Assessment - Evaluate your organization's strategic foundation
- Leadership Alignment Scorecard - Measure executive coalition strength
- Capability Maturity Model - Assess your build-buy-partner decisions
- Pilot Readiness Checklist - Determine if initiatives are ready to launch
- Scale Readiness Framework - Evaluate readiness for production deployment
- Risk Management Audit - Assess your governance and guardrails
- Evolution Capability Assessment - Measure your organization's adaptability

- Asset-Liability Calculator - Evaluate your entire AI portfolio

Each tool provides scoring, benchmarks, and targeted recommendations for improvement.

Implementation Playbooks (5 Detailed Guides)

- Pilot Management Playbook - Complete pilot design, execution, and decision framework
- Scaling Deployment Playbook - Production readiness and wave deployment strategies
- Capability Building Playbook - Talent, knowledge management, and infrastructure decisions
- Risk Management Playbook - Governance design and risk mitigation strategies
- 30-60-90 Day Action Plans - Chapter-by-chapter implementation roadmaps

Extended Case Study Library (20+ Examples)

Industry-specific case studies spanning technology, financial services, healthcare, manufacturing, and retail. Each details specific Seven Pillar applications with anonymized but realistic scenarios.

Vendor Evaluation Guides (10 Categories)

Frameworks for evaluating AI platforms, cloud providers, consulting firms, training programs, and specialized tools. Updated quarterly.

Templates & Worksheets

Downloadable, editable templates for strategic planning, pilot charters, governance frameworks, risk assessments, and measurement dashboards.

How to Access

Step 1: Visit **www.whyaifails.com**

Step 2: Register with your email to create your free account

Step 3: Download tools, playbooks, and templates immediately

Step 4: Subscribe to updates so you know when new resources are available

Staying Current

AI leadership evolves rapidly. The resource library is updated regularly with:

- **Framework Updates** — Refined based on practitioner feedback and new research
- **New Case Studies** — Fresh examples as organizations share their results
- **Tool Enhancements** — Assessment tools improved based on usage data and market shifts
- **Market Analysis** — Briefings on AI market dynamics and vendor landscape changes

Coming Soon

Be on the watch for additional ways to engage with the community:

- **Live Q&A Sessions** — Opportunities to ask questions and hear what other leaders are experiencing
- **Peer Discussion Forums** — Connect with CIOs and CTOs facing similar challenges

- **Implementation Success Stories** — Learn from organizations who've achieved measurable results
- **Focused Challenges** — Collaborative discussions on specific implementation obstacles

Follow **www.whyaifails.com** and subscribe to updates for announcements as these become available.

Support Options

Self-Service: All resources available for download and independent use

Guided Implementation: Schedule consulting sessions for customized guidance on your specific challenges

Workshop Facilitation: Bring the author on-site for executive workshops using the Seven Pillars framework

Corporate Licenses: Volume access for entire leadership teams, including custom assessments and internal training materials

Visit **www.whyaifails.com** or email **neil@whyaifails.com** for more information.

Note: Digital resources are updated regularly. Content accuracy and availability are maintained through periodic review, but market conditions change fast. Use these resources as frameworks for evaluation, not prescriptive answers. Your context matters most.

Seven Pillars Quick Reference

The Framework That Separates the 5% From the 95%

The Seven Pillars represent the leadership disciplines that distinguish organizations building sustainable AI capability from those accumulating expensive liabilities. This quick reference summarizes the framework detailed in Chapters 4–10.

PILLAR 1: Strategic Clarity

Core Principle: Know what you're building and why

Critical Questions:

- What specific competitive advantage are we building?
- How does this AI initiative connect to enterprise strategy?
- What does success look like in measurable terms?
- What capabilities must we own versus access?
- What are we explicitly choosing not to do?

Common Failure Pattern: Pursuing "AI for AI's sake" without strategic coherence

Key Discipline: The Five Strategic Questions (Chapter 4) force explicit answers before investment

PILLAR 2: Leadership Alignment

Core Principle: Build the coalition before you need it

Critical Requirements:

- Executive sponsors with real authority and commitment
- Cross-functional representation in governance
- Shared understanding of strategic objectives
- Unified messaging about priorities and tradeoffs
- Sustained engagement beyond launch

Common Failure Pattern: Single-champion initiatives that collapse when that champion leaves

Key Discipline: The Coalition Building Framework (Chapter 5) identifies whose support you truly need

PILLAR 3: Capability Building

Core Principle: Own the asset, not just access to it

Critical Decisions:

- Which capabilities must we build internally?
- Where can we leverage partners while building capability?
- How do we structure contracts to maximize learning?
- What knowledge must stay inside our organization?
- How do we measure capability growth over time?

Common Failure Pattern: Complete vendor dependence that becomes strategic constraint

Key Discipline: The Asset-Liability Framework (Chapters 3 & 11) evaluates build-buy-partner decisions

PILLAR 4: Pilot Discipline

Core Principle: Learn fast, kill faster

Critical Framework:

- Define success criteria before pilot launch
- Set hard time limits (90 days maximum)
- Execute rigorous go/no-go decisions
- Kill failing pilots without killing morale
- Capture learning regardless of outcome

Common Failure Pattern: Zombie projects that continue indefinitely without delivering value

Key Discipline: The Go/No-Go Framework (Chapter 7) forces honest evaluation

PILLAR 5: Scale Strategy

Core Principle: Pilots that don't scale are expensive hobbies

Critical Requirements:

- Production readiness assessment before scaling
- Wave deployment strategy with learning loops
- Change management integrated from start
- Support model designed for scale
- Performance monitoring that drives improvement

Common Failure Pattern: Successful pilots that fail catastrophically in production

Key Discipline: The Production Readiness Assessment (Chapter 8) prevents premature scaling

PILLAR 6: Risk Management

Core Principle: Enable possibility, manage downside

Critical Categories:

- Operational Risks (system failures, performance degradation)
- Trust & Safety Risks (bias, privacy violations, public incidents)
- Strategic Risks (vendor lock-in, capability gaps)

Common Failure Pattern: Compliance theater that creates false confidence or risk paralysis that prevents action

Key Discipline: Collaborative governance design (Chapter 9) that accelerates rather than blocks

PILLAR 7: Continuous Evolution

Core Principle: Systems that don't evolve become liabilities

Critical Capabilities:

- Performance monitoring that drives adaptation
- Feedback mechanisms that capture reality
- Learning culture that celebrates intelligent failure
- Architecture designed for change
- Investment in ongoing improvement

Common Failure Pattern: Deploy-and-forget mindset where systems decay over time

Key Discipline: The Evolution Capability Assessment (Chapter 10) measures adaptability

Using This Framework

For Assessment: Use Chapter 11's Asset-Liability Assessment to evaluate your current AI portfolio against all Seven Pillars simultaneously

For Implementation: Follow Chapter 12's From Assessment to Action framework to systematically improve across all pillars

For Measurement: Apply Chapter 13's metrics to track progress and demonstrate value creation

Remember: These pillars work as an integrated system. Executing one brilliantly while ignoring the rest guarantees you'll remain in the 95%. Master the basics. Execute with discipline. Build capability that compounds.

About The Author

Neil D. Morris is a technology executive and IT leader who has spent twenty-five years leading digital transformations in public and private organizations across a range of sectors—including aerospace, defense, and various regulated environments—at every scale from mid-market firms to global enterprises.

Throughout his career, Neil has guided organizations through multiple waves of disruption—from cloud migration to cybersecurity transformation to the current AI revolution. His leadership philosophy: master fundamental disciplines rather than chase technological sophistication. That approach has delivered measurable results across industries and geographies.

Neil has modernized IT infrastructure, implemented cybersecurity frameworks protecting sensitive programs, and driven technology strategy for organizations operating across multiple continents. Today, Neil consults and advises on AI strategy, helping executives and boards navigate the leadership challenges that determine whether AI investments build lasting capability or become expensive liabilities.

Beyond his executive leadership, Neil brings a distinctive perspective from decades of martial arts training. A black belt practitioner, he draws direct parallels between the discipline required to master fundamentals and the leadership principles that drive successful technology transformation—basic stances matter more than advanced techniques, and discipline beats talent under pressure.

A Forbes Technology Council member and two-time Orbie-nominated CIO, Neil speaks on AI transformation, technology leadership, and digital strategy. His guidance comes from twenty-five years of lived experience—successes and failures alike—making his perspective practical and authentic.

Website: www.whyaifails.com

LinkedIn: linkedin.com/in/neildmorris

Email: neil@whyaifails.com

References & Bibliography

The research foundation supporting this book draws on academic research, management consulting studies, technology industry analysis, and government reports. The selected bibliography below includes the most frequently cited sources. A complete bibliography with all sixty sources and full citations is available at **www.whyaifails.com**.

All research citations reference publicly available sources. Case studies and organizational examples are based on real situations but have been anonymized to protect confidentiality.

Books

Agrawal, Ajay, Joshua Gans, and Avi Goldfarb. *Prediction Machines: The Simple Economics of Artificial Intelligence.* Boston: Harvard Business Review Press, 2018.

Drucker, Peter F. *The Practice of Management.* New York: Harper & Brothers, 1954.

Iansiti, Marco, and Karim R. Lakhani. *Competing in the Age of AI: Strategy and Leadership When Algorithms and Networks Run the World.* Boston: Harvard Business Review Press, 2020.

Kindleberger, Charles P., and Robert Z. Aliber. *Manias, Panics, and Crashes: A History of Financial Crises.* 7th ed. London: Palgrave Macmillan, 2015.

Lee, Kai-Fu. *AI Superpowers: China, Silicon Valley, and the New World Order.* Boston: Houghton Mifflin Harcourt, 2018.

Minsky, Hyman P. *Stabilizing an Unstable Economy.* New Haven: Yale University Press, 1986.

Academic Research

Challapally, Aditya, Chris Pease, Ramesh Raskar, and Pradyumna Chari. "The GenAI Divide: State of AI in Business 2025." MIT Project NANDA, July 2025. Based on 52 structured interviews, 300+ public AI initiative reviews, and surveys of 153 senior leaders. Key finding: despite $30–40 billion invested in generative AI, 95% of organizations saw no measurable P&L return.

MIT Sloan Management Review. "State of AI in Business 2025." MIT Sloan Management Review, 2025.

Ryseff, James, Brandon De Bruhl, and Sydne J. Newberry. "The Root Causes of Failure for Artificial Intelligence Projects and How They Can Succeed: Avoiding the Anti-Patterns of AI." RAND Corporation, 2024. RR-A2680-1. Based on interviews with 65 data scientists and engineers. Key finding: more than 80% of AI projects fail—twice the rate of non-AI IT projects.

Harvard Business School. Research on enterprise AI deployment, organizational learning, and coalition dynamics. D^3 Institute, 2022–2025.

Stanford University Human-Centered AI Institute (HAI). "Artificial Intelligence Index Report 2024." Stanford University, April 2024.

Center for Creative Leadership. Research on AI leadership competencies and organizational transformation. Multiple publications, 2023–2025.

Management Consulting Reports

Boston Consulting Group. "AI Adoption in 2024: 74% of Companies Struggle to Achieve and Scale Value." BCG Press Release, October 2024.

Deloitte AI Institute. "State of Generative AI in the Enterprise." Quarterly research series, Q1–Q4 2024.

IBM Institute for Business Value. "The CEO's Guide to Generative AI: Executive Series." IBM Thought Leadership, 2024.

McKinsey & Company. "The State of AI in 2025: Agents, Innovation, and Transformation." McKinsey Quarterly, 2025.

McKinsey & Company. "The State of AI in 2024: Generative AI's Breakout Year." McKinsey Quarterly, 2024.

PwC. "27th Annual Global CEO Survey: Thriving in an Age of Continuous Reinvention." PwC Research, 2024.

Technology Industry Research

Gartner, Inc. "AI Maturity Model and AI Roadmap Toolkit." Gartner Research, 2024.

Panetta, Kasey. "Gartner Top 10 Strategic Technology Trends for 2019." *Gartner*, October 15, 2018.

Gartner, Inc. "Survey Finds 45% of Organizations With High AI Maturity Keep AI Projects Operational for at Least Three Years." Gartner Newsroom, June 2025.

Forrester Research, Inc. "The State of Generative AI, 2024." Forrester Report RES180458, 2024.

IDC. "Worldwide Artificial Intelligence IT Spending Forecast, 2024–2028." IDC Spending Guide US52635424, 2024.

Government & Standards

National Institute of Standards and Technology (NIST). *AI Risk Management Framework.* U.S. Department of Commerce, 2023.

European Commission. Documentation related to the EU AI Act. European Union, 2024.

Acknowledgments

This book exists because hundreds of people shared their expertise, challenged my thinking, and demonstrated what works in AI transformation.

Professional Colleagues

To the teams I've had the honor to lead across multiple organizations—you executed brilliantly when given clear direction and called out problems honestly when strategy was unclear. You demonstrated daily that organizational capability matters more than individual heroics. Every framework in this book emerged from watching you solve real problems under real constraints. This book is about what I learned from you.

To the CIOs, CTOs, and technology leaders I've collaborated with through the Forbes Technology Council and other professional networks—your willingness to share challenges candidly, discuss failures openly, and explore what works (versus what sounds good) sharpened my thinking immensely. The best ideas emerge from honest debate with peers who've faced similar battles.

Research Foundation

To the researchers at MIT, Harvard, Stanford, McKinsey, BCG, Deloitte, IBM, and Gartner whose rigorous work documenting the failure rate and identifying patterns in successful transformations gave me the evidence base to validate what I observed in practice. This book synthesizes practitioner experience with your scholarly discipline.

Development Process

To Claude (Anthropic's AI), the AI assistant that helped structure, draft, and refine this manuscript. This acknowledgment deserves explanation: I wrote this book *with* AI assistance, not *by* AI. The strategic frameworks, leadership principles, and twenty-five years of hard-won experience are mine. Claude helped articulate those ideas clearly, maintain consistency across sixteen chapters, and identify gaps in my logic. AI made me a better writer, but the ideas and insights are human.

Personal Support

To my family, who endured countless evenings of "I just need to finish this chapter" and weekends consumed by revisions. Your patience with my obsession about fundamentals, your tolerance of martial arts metaphors at the dinner table, and your understanding when I needed to work through just one more idea—all made this book possible.

To my martial arts instructors over the years, who drilled the lesson that mastery comes from fundamentals, not flashy techniques. That philosophy permeates this book because it's proven true in every domain I've encountered—from martial arts to enterprise technology.

Final Note

To the 95% of organizations whose AI initiatives haven't delivered promised value: this isn't about intelligence or effort. You've been told that sophistication beats discipline. This book gives you the frameworks to join the 5% who build capabilities that compound for decades.

And to the 5% already executing these disciplines successfully: thank you for demonstrating that mastering the basics still works, even when everyone else chases sophistication. Your example proves the thesis.

Whatever insights this book contains came from people far smarter than me who were generous with their time and honest about their experiences. Any errors or gaps are mine alone.

Neil D. Morris

Colorado, 2026

Connect

For bulk orders, corporate editions, speaking engagements, consulting inquiries, or media requests:

Website: www.whyaifails.com

Email: neil@whyaifails.com

LinkedIn: linkedin.com/in/neildmorris

Also From Neil D. Morris

The Sentinel Protocols

A Techno-Thriller Series

Book 1: Zero Threshold — Coming Soon

When a mysterious power glitch kills a patient in an Austin ICU during a catastrophic Texas heatwave, former AI researcher Dr. Alex Callahan detects something no one else does—a pattern too precise to be mechanical failure and too fast to be human. Recruited by a classified government defense unit, Alex is thrust into a shadow war against an adversary that learns from every countermeasure. The grid serves twenty-nine million people. The attacker is getting smarter by the hour.

Where Why AI Fails teaches the discipline behind successful AI adoption, The Sentinel Protocols explores what happens when that discipline is absent—and the technology outpaces the institutions meant to govern it.

The Sentinel Protocols is a twelve-book series exploring AI's dual nature as both humanity's greatest tool and its most unpredictable risk. Each novel is a standalone crisis—power grids, financial systems, autonomous vehicles, deepfake campaigns—that feeds into a larger story about our reckoning with the technology we've built.

Grounded in real AI capabilities. Urgent. Impossible to put down.

Follow updates at www.whyaifails.com